Notes from an Old Fly Book

for the dear
Rosensteins, their
visit to us in Boulder
& our walk on the mall
With all attention

Gordon
June 15, 2002

CAHILL PINK LADY MARCH BROWN QUILL GORDON RIO GRANDE KING COACHMAN DUSTY MILLER GINGER QUILL BLACK GNAT HENDRICKSON GRIZZLY KING HARE'S EAR

The Major Pitcher

Notes from an Old
FLY BOOK

Gordon M. Wickstrom

[signature]

University Press of Colorado

Published by the University Press of Colorado
5589 Arapahoe Avenue, Suite 206C
Boulder, Colorado 80303

The University Press of Colorado is a cooperative publishing enterprise supported, in part, by Adams State College, Colorado State University, Fort Lewis College, Mesa State College, Metropolitan State College of Denver, University of Colorado, University of Northern Colorado, University of Southern Colorado, and Western State College of Colorado.

The paper used in this publication meets the minimum requirements of the American National Standard for Information Sciences—Permanence of Paper for Printed Library Materials. ANSI Z39.48-1992

Illustration credits: p. 8—Larry Largay (courtesy *Fly Tyer*); p. 10—John Betts; p. 20—Phoenix Lines (www.phoenixlines.com); p. 23—from *McClane's New Standard Fishing Encyclopedia and International Angling Guide, Enlarged and Revised,* by A. J. McClane, illustrated by Richard E. Younger and Frances Watkins. Copyright, © 1974 by A. J. McClane (reprinted by permission of Henry Holt & Co., LLC); p. 40—J. R. Tomelleri; p. 125—from *The Gothic Image: Religious Art in the Thirteenth Century* by Emile Male, 1973 (reprinted with permission from Perseus Books Group); p. 135—Gustave Courbet, "La truite," 1871 (© 2001 Kunsthaus Zurich. All rights reserved.); p. 174—Richard L. Henry and Clarence Reichard

Portions of this book were originally printed in *Reel News, The American Fly Fisher, Gray's Sporting Journal, Angler's Journal, Journal of Irish Literature,* and *Scenic and Majestic.*

Every reasonable effort has been made to trace the ownership of all copyrighted material included in this book. Any errors that may have occurred are inadvertent and will be corrected in subsequent editions, provided that notification is sent to the publisher.

Library of Congress Cataloging-in-Publication Data

Wickstrom, Gordon M., 1926–
     Notes from an old fly book / Gordon M. Wickstrom.
          p. cm.
     ISBN 0-87081-613-6 (alk. paper)
       1. Fly-fishing—Front Range (Colo. and Wyoming) I. Title.
SH464.F76 W53 2001
799.1'24'097886—dc21

                                        2001035599

Cover design by Laura Furney
Text design by Daniel Pratt

10 09 08 07 06 05 04 03 02 01   10 9 8 7 6 5 4 3 2 1

For the grandchildren—

Linnea's
Per Maresca
and
Maurya's
Erin and Naoise Reynolds

Contents

Thinking About It

Some of It in Verse

Foreword

Gordon Wickstrom and I have accumulated over one hundred years on the water. Although we'd have had it otherwise, it is now close to the end of that time that we have become friends, begun our long conversations, and fished together. Among the things we have talked about is the paradox in fly casting, the special, perhaps unique, physical connection between angler and fly necessary to achieve distance and accuracy but at the same time restrict them. This intimate physical connection of angler to the fly in fly fishing is crucial and of unparalleled fascination.

Weightless flies are propelled through unseen and unpredictable vagaries of the air to within inches of trout, yards away. We don't know the exact distance, nor can we see the backcast, which is half of the casting cycle that must be made. The cast just happens all at once, in very little time, and on most occasions without a hitch. The exhilaration of that moment, thinking about it, memories of it, is one of the reasons we do it over and over.

When reading Gordon's *Notes From an Old Fly Book* or his little quarterly, "The Bouldercreek Angler," you must read with care. On the surface, the essays, poems, and stories are about fishing in the Rocky Mountains where the water is bright and full of life. But Gordon is also capable of isolating and penetrating an idea, plumbing its depths while remaining connected to that idea's place within something larger. Descending through the layers, he replaces ordinary shapes with dark and sometimes disturbing ideas and images. The lines of Gordon's thought are laid out back and forth, making their points on both old and new questions about fishing and his own life in it. Some casts are made to places that are safe and free of snags, while others go to places more perilous. The ability to see and explain this to others comes from Gordon's long experience, training, and discipline.

In this book we encounter the "tragic human fix," the fix we have made for ourselves by our removal by technology from what was once natural to us. Gordon also delves into the pastoral myth, the belief that life and sport are better out there in the country than here in the city. We cling to a sense of continuity with a bucolic past, keeping it distinct from the modern environment we have created around us. We dismiss the frustrations and trying moments of a fishing trip, because at one time or another we have all had the feeling that the one good day made all of the rest of it worthwhile. When we return home, we may remember that the high point was the day it didn't rain.

Anglers have often wished to record every moment of a great fishing trip, but when they do, they also stir up those unpleasant things as well. Would we keep dozens of images of the crude fumblings between angler and fish in the practice of catch and release? Wouldn't we edit our memories to eliminate all this? We prefer to hold onto the pastoral myth by keeping uppermost in memory moments like the imagined transformation of those dying sunfish in Gordon's concluding essay, "Ghost Lake."

We are linked to our past by a veil hanging between our survival and extinction, between finding food or perishing. Fishing reenacts this crisis, where instinctive decisions will determine whether we symbolically survive or perish.

It is a singular moment. The trout's rise to a fly floating toward its future is the acceptance of our fly-as-*amulet*. The presentation of this amulet is *hope sent into uncertainty*. If it is rejected, the veil between life and death remains intact and we are at risk. In order for us to live, the fly must be taken.

Gordon and I have often talked of what we had to go through years ago to meet the conditions we found on the stream. As a boy in Boulder during the Great Depression, he tied flies for local anglers for little or nothing. *Use it up, wear it out, make it do, or do without* has disappeared from our popular philosophies. Anglers today will readily buy new equipment instead of making what's needed or learning a new way to use what is already at hand. It is no wonder that readily available answers are popular—they are easier and safer. What is lost is the depth of comprehension that comes from regular and sustained practice.

The order of life that Gordon illustrates in his book is like that of the order of the flies in the books and boxes we each carry. These flies have been taken out, used, put back in, lost and replaced. Some of them were put there long ago alongside new ones tied in anticipation of fishing trips yet to come. Even if in a jumble, these flies are a kind of personal record of the angler's life, and a shorthand for the complex history of angling as well. Their order is always changing, always fascinating, full of affecting memory—and often surprising.

Gordon's invitation to have a part in this book has been a daunting experience. It is one of the privileges of my life to know something of his kindness, sense of humanity, clear thought, civility, and love of life in which fly fishing has played such a role.

So, read his *Notes* with care. They are more than just *about* fly fishing. As he suggests in his graphic display "The History of Fishing for Trout with Artificial Flies," "Fly fishing can be imagined as the *material expression* of its literature"—of books like this.

—*John Betts*

Preface

A number of these essays began as a regular column in the newsletter of the Boulder, Colorado, chapter of Trout Unlimited. Others have appeared in various angling journals—*The American Fly Fisher, Gray's Sporting Journal, Angler's Journal, The Fly Tyer*—and a few of them nowhere until now.

They began as an effort to record what I remembered of trout fishing along the Front Range of the Colorado Rockies, focusing on what was then the sleepy, small university town of Boulder some sixty years ago, and to vent a few ideas about what I think fishing is and who the angler might be in the larger scheme of things. I wanted to tell several stories that amused me, honor some treasured memories, and, perhaps most of all, risk a look beneath the conventional and surface complacencies of the sport. Some of my musings became verse.

I wanted to leave a paper trail of an old grandfather for three still-small grandchildren that they might one day discover a trout stream of their own and know what to do with it.

I smile to think that fifty-plus years ago, I fantasized about being a fishing writer for the magazines, fishing all over the place, all the time, with all those famous fishermen. But an academic career swept me away from Boulder Creek and into a life of making and teaching theatre. "A fisherman who teaches school and stages plays" was my self-definition. And now here, these many years later, after teaching, after making plays for more than forty years, I'm a bit of a fishing writer after all. It dazzles me. Were our lives revealed to us in advance, we'd never believe it.

I am struck by how writing narrowly about fishing paradoxically has allowed me to speak about the broader issues of my life and experience, about art, and especially about language itself. It only goes to show how deep and abiding the metaphor of the fish and the fisherman is after all. The literature of angling is so vast, detailed, and powerful, especially in English (there are said to have been 4,848 books on fishing published in English before 1920), that I've ventured to maintain that fishing is, in fact, the material expression of that literature. It is as though the literature came first and created the angler. As though fly fishing in particular is the creature of the English language. Which means that I'm not at all sure whether the literature describes my angling or my angling is a response to the literature. In any case, the literature of angling has surely driven the sport over its five centuries of record.

The pieces that I here presume to add to the great mass of writing about fishing are various in form, content, and tone. Whatever else they may be, they are certainly not imaginative literature, literature as art. The best that I, and writers like me, can hope is that our writing may fit in someplace between literature and daily journalism. I do hope, however, that this book may become part of the record of angling that now, in my retirement, I profess as critic and ancient enthusiast. Somehow this new role doesn't feel too far removed from my previous life as a professor of drama and its literature.

In the belief that no one's reputation was ever ruined by brevity, I have kept each of these pieces to only a few minutes' reading, some shorter even than that. For me, they combine into something like an *apologia* within the mysteries and pleasures, even the frustrations, of it all. They track both joy and sorrow and a few, maybe, a perversity.

Whatever they may or may not be, or mean, they are for those three grandchildren whom I shall never know beyond their early childhood, but whom I shall always find some way or other to love.

About this Book

The reader of these essays is certain, several times, to run afoul of the expression "back then." This calling up the past—is it merely the ravings of an old troglodyte yearning for the past that never really was, the rawest sort of nostalgia as antidote to present fears and horrible imaginings?

Guilty as I am of presuming to set up my memory as privileged, let me try to distance myself from personal investment and delve into a more general fund of memory. I am indebted to David Cole and his study of the processes of theatre for the Latin term *Illud Tempus,* meaning roughly "back then"—a past event of archetypal power—in other words, a highly charged "back then." Not the junk memories stuffing our heads, but the recall of moments that have had a common and determinate force in our culture, even in our history as a species. In religion these are memories of the signal events that we honor in ritual and ceremony concerning ultimate things. In angling they are necessarily much much less, but still solid determinants in our experience of our dear sport. I hope my recollections of the history of angling with a fly are not peculiar to me, but part of our collective history as anglers—our *Illud Tempus.*

These memories ought to be signposts that have pointed the way. They ought to be the models we depend on in order to identify what a fisherman is deep down. They ought to be the bases upon which we know it is safe and decent to expend emotion. They are assurances of continuity, these necessary memories of ourselves "back then," even if we weren't there "back then."

The memorial information and critical analyses in these pages may seem to the skeptical reader rather too highly localized in person and place. But perhaps there can emerge from it all a general application. Hamlet, a case in point and arguably the most particularized and localized character in our experience, literary or otherwise, becomes the most universal, most fully revealed image of a human being that we know of—by virtue of our remembering him through the work of the actor onstage or the word on the page.

Back then, when we were kids, we used to say, "What's all that got to do with the price of beans in Russia?" Indeed, what has all this to do with fishing the fly? It seems to me, what with the tremendous burgeoning of fly fishing in the last quarter century, that we have run roughshod over the top of our history, tradition, lore, and theory. We have come close to forgetting it. Only now has a shy curiosity and need appeared, especially among young anglers, for reconnection—dare I say, for the discovery of the *Illud Tempi* of angling.

Any number of angling writers are now sharing in this effort at reconstruction through personal recall and scholarship. And none too soon. Historical literacy is on the wane, memory too often consigned to the merely cybernetic. There is only this little moment when a modest but gratifying interest in the past has expressed itself and ought to be satisfied.

When I was working on my graphic display "The History of Fishing for Trout With Artificial Flies in Britain and America," it was John Betts, that canniest of thinkers, craftsmen, and artists when it comes to fishing, who urged me to include William Caxton. In the fifteenth century, Caxton, using movable type, printed the first book in English and made possible the printing and publication in 1496 of *The Treatyse of Fysshynge With an Angle,* that work most fundamental to all subsequent fly fishing.

At this singular moment in the history of language, printing, and publication, the English set about becoming inveterate readers of secular books, getting the jump—and holding on to it—over the rest of Europe in matters literary and sporting.

This turning point, when Caxton and his colleague, Wynken de Worde, who printed the *Treatyse,* changed their world with the printing press, is surely a profound example of "back then."

And so in that spirit and with the saving grace of memory, I present these essays as a share in the effort to recover, within the tensions, doubts, and complexities of present circumstances, our "back then." Though this book may seem to focus on a small geography, Colorado's Front Range, I hope that, like Hamlet's Elsinore, it will resonate with a wider significance for our sport.

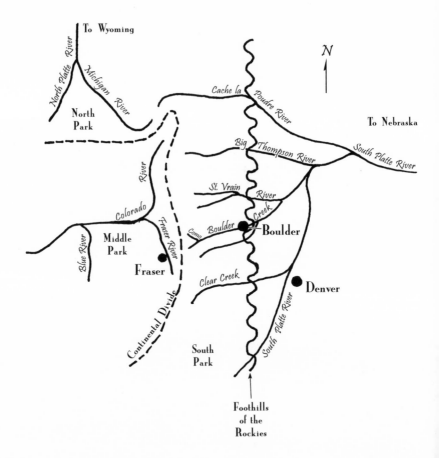

Flies in the Book
and Other Tackle

Treasure

The family gathering after Uncle Clarence's funeral was still going strong when I, in my fourteenth year, drifted away from all that strange high-spiritedness that often follows a family funeral and wandered out to the shed in back, where I found treasure: Uncle Clarence's fishing tackle.

There was his Granger Champion fly rod and a badly worn creel stuffed with all his gear, including his brittle old fly book, just as he'd left it after his last trip to North Park, where real, grown-up fishermen in those days went on real, grown-up fishing trips.

A few days later, I shyly told my aunt about my discovery. She must have sensed how dearly I would have loved to have any of that cache of tackle, so much finer and more complete than my own gear, because she smiled and told me it was all mine. That beautiful cane rod and the treasures of the old creel, broken down from the weight of the many trout it had borne home and still smelling of those same old dead trout, were talismans of a mysterious and wonderful world that I longed to enter as a serious fisherman.

But about that old fly book stuffed with both new and bedraggled flies, two or three spinners, leaders, snelled hooks, a fishing license. I felt about it then as I still feel about any angler's fly box—that it was an especially private place, like a personal diary, that I had no business prying into. Still, Uncle Clarence was safely dead, and here was his fly book in my hands, no longer his private property. I put aside my uneasy sense of intruding and probed the book carefully, rather as I now do the ideas in these essays.

The flies were all wets, nearly all size 10, and snelled to six inches of gut, all quite similar in profile, most of them with wings of duck-quill slips, heavy with hackle, and bearing little resemblance to anything in nature. They were traditional patterns, many of them of English ancestry, now become steadfastly western American.

As far as anything in nature goes, the living insects we saw a-stream back in those days we called either gnats or mosquitoes. Such was our entomology in 1940. I look back on it with something like grief, thinking, *If only I knew then what I know now. If only I had the tackle then that I have now—and knew how to use it.*

I recall that everyone I knew or had heard of back then, like Uncle Clarence, fished with flies, but none, I think, would have called himself a fly fisherman. It was simply nature's way that one fished worms and spinners in the early season when the streams were high and turbid. When the waters dropped and cleared, though, the old anglers unself-consciously turned to their flies. I hasten to add that fishing—with flies or anything else—was not considered at all fashionable.

Those standard old flies in the standard old fly book— now such a pleasure to recall—were sold from boxes of twelve at two for a quarter. Any town of any size within reach of the mountains could boast of several places to buy them. On the road, in the mountains, basic flies, as well as other essentials of tackle, were available in most filling stations and drugstores.

If, perhaps, one had heard of dry flies, or more unlikely yet, the arcane nymph, that angler would have had to go to Denver or comb the catalogs to find them. Ours was a wet-fly culture. And we were content.

Those old wet flies, in those trout-fragrant fly books, have wonderful names, fine-sounding names, names to make one hum with pleasure. Let me list the treasury of flies as Uncle

Clarence and the storekeepers knew them. Let
me read from a fine old fly book a litany of them
in memory of fishing days past.

A Litany
Read and Listen!

Rio Grande King; Western Bee; Captain; Coach-
man; Royal Coachman; Lead-winged Coachman;
Cowdung; Blue Bottle; Jock Scott; Silver Doctor;
Wickham's Fancy; McGinty; Greenwell's Glory;
Blue Quill; Ginger Quill; Black Gnat; the Grey
Hackles—yellow, red, green, and peacock;
Grizzly King; Gold-Ribbed Hare's Ear; White
Miller; Yellow Sally; Badger Palmer; Blue Dun;
California Hackle; the Brown Hackles—peacock,
red, and yellow; Flight's Fancy; Professor; Pink
Lady; Mosquito; Montreal; Queen of Waters;
King of Waters; Red Ant; Black Ant; March
Brown; Cahills, light and dark; Rube Wood;
Red Ibis; Governor; Parmachene Belle; Blue
Upright; Whirling Blue Dun; Warden's Worry;
Willow; Dusty Miller; Seth Green; Deer Fly;
Iron Blue Dun; Mormon Girl; Major Pitcher;
and the fabled Pott hair flies, the Mite family—
Sandy, Buddy, Dina, Mister, and Lady Mite.

We'd pore over those old fly books the way a
nun, longing for grace, might tell her beads.

Classic Wet Flies

I've been preoccupied with the old wet flies. Perhaps it's only a bout with nostalgia, but whatever the reason for this delving into the past, my own past, it's a pleasant relief from trying to keep up with the relentless stream of flies emerging from today's "new dispensation" in trout fishing.

This is a golden age of fly tying and fly fishing. The daring, the imagination, the skill of today's fly tiers is a wonder to behold. Each new pattern is—or claims to be—more effective with trout than the last. The new flies really work, proving that we anglers are clearly smarter than the trout after all. That's some consolation.

I've long held that the last crafty old brown trout left swimming our waters will fall prey to an artificial fly, probably a pattern not yet conceived, one that that wary old fish absolutely cannot resist.

That ultimate fly, that dressing for the apocalypse, won't look much like my fond old wet flies. The trend over the past, let's say, forty years has been steadily toward ever smaller, drabber, minimalist flies that come closer and closer to the appearance and action in the water of real insects. One can hardly remember the names of these new flies, so drab, colorless, and devoid of personality are their names and often their construction. Of course we have to remember that there is also a new generation of big, sometimes spectacular, attractor flies that represent nothing at all in nature, yet often bring up the most stubborn fish.

The new flies that directly represent insect life are now the bread-and-butter of our angling. They may lack the glamour of the big, modern attractors and may be a far cry in visual appeal from the old-time "fancy" wet flies, but they are superb fish takers. I'm quite convinced that those old wet flies, with their wonderful antique names would be relatively ineffective when fished over today's more sophisticated, heavily pressured trout. The new dispensation in flies must win the laurel of utility hands down. They catch even the most difficult fish regularly.

But, as with most things, interest in old ways returns, however briefly, to enjoy a vogue among the new generation. And those of us seasoned enough to remember "back then" suddenly have something to say. Now is a time of remembering. The articles about the old flies, and fishing them, in the many fly-fishing magazines point up this interest and exploit it.

The dominant characteristic of these great old flies is their often flamboyant wing, commonly cut from a duck-wing flight quill. As these flies have been so long out of fashion, few of the younger tiers have learned the tricky matter of tying them. We old-timers, however, can still do it—and with pleasure.

Returning to my origins as a fly tier, I've lately tied a representative collection of fifty of the old dressings in a thoroughly classical manner, the manner of that master of the wet fly James E. Leisenring. The flies are on display before me now as I write, with their brilliant bodies of raw silk floss or dubbed fur, often ribbed with gold or silver tinsel, their softly sparse and delicate hackles veiling the body, and each one flying that banner of a wing, sometimes rising up, sometimes lying low over the body. Most are like nothing ever seen in nature: there's the Silver Doctor, the Jock Scott, the Parmachene Belle, and the Red Ibis among the really fancy flies, as well as the more sober Grey Hackle Yellow, Iron Blue Dun, Grizzly King, and Ginger Quill—flies a little more like naturals.

These old flies have a long and complicated history. Many are of English origin, some of them American, and a few of western American development, all of them variations on a theme. One of the most famous western flies, with, I think, the grandest of names, is the Rio Grande King, special, of course, to Colorado. With a Grey Hackle Yellow, the Rio Grande King made up what was one of the most common casts along the Colorado Front Range.

Tracing the histories of these flies can become a passion in itself.

But whatever their origin, they are a pleasure to sit and look at and rehearse their names. Trout flies are a justification unto themselves, rife with fascinating lore, infinite in variety and subtlety. These old flies also have the appeal of wanting almost wholly natural materials—silk, fur, and feather—in contrast to the many synthetic materials deployed in today's new dispensation of trout flies.

Here now, as a gentle and fond remembrance of things past, are these old-time wet flies, newly emerged from my vise and sparkling here on my bench. They'll never get wet, never lure a trout. They must be preserved. They exist for their own sake—or maybe for those grandchildren, one day, when as artifacts of the past they may still to have the power to lure that new generation into dreams of another time and place, of splendid rivers and streams, of numinous trout to whom flies like these once were cast—and often taken.

The Major Pitcher

Tail: lemon wood duck.
Body: yellow silk floss rear half;
red silk floss front half.
Hackle: palmered furnace.
Wing: white duck quill slips
with narrow cheek of Silver Doctor
blue swan up each side of wing.
Hook: size 10 sproat, snelled.

Numberless were the old wet flies that sported bright, colorful, often exotic plumage and silks. Endlessly fanciful, these flies came, in fact, to be called "fancy" flies. Nowhere are these beautiful artifacts of the last century and before better illustrated than in the plates of Ray Bergman's *Trout* (1938) and Mary Orvis Marbury's seminal *Favorite Flies and Their Histories* of 1892).[1] These flies speak of early times, of only gentle fishing pressure, and of the naiveté of the eastern brook trout. They have little to do with insects found in nature, but much to do with the pleasures of the fly tier's and angler's imagination.

In 1942, one of these fancy flies mysteriously found its way to Boulder. It was the Major Pitcher, a beautiful, rather complicated wet fly, suddenly in great demand by local anglers. How it came to town, I hadn't the least idea. It wasn't to be found in any local store.

I had tied flies for a couple of years and had acquired the basic skills; so when my mentor and fly-tying employer E. B. Edwards (I scrubbed the floors of his tackle/jewelry shop once a week) declared that he wouldn't tie the difficult Major Pitcher, he handed his orders over to me. I tied them and hated it—at fifty cents the dozen.

The Major Pitcher
Painting by John Betts

The pattern was slow and tough to tie well, what with its bicolor silk body, its palmered hackle and white duck wing with that strip of blue swan flank feather up each side of the wing, so stubborn to make lie just right. And I had to snell them into the bargain. I would much rather have been tying the ever popular Rio Grande Kings and Gray Hackle Yellows.

Kids ought to be more curious about the origins of such things, but they aren't. I wish I had been curious about the Major Pitcher craze. Looking back now, it all seems quite extraordinary. I remember assuming that the fly, fancy as it was, had something to do with major-league baseball. The red, white, and blue in the dressing suggested something national, perhaps the National League. And that word, *pitcher.* Such was the beginning and end of my youthful speculation.

Then, after four decades of occasional musings on my experience with the Major Pitcher—there was always one in my wet-fly box—I came upon the fall 1974 issue of that excellent publication *The American Fly Fisher.* There I read that the pattern was named for turn-of-the-century Yellowstone National Park acting superintendent Major John Pitcher, much admired for advancing the cause of the park's trout.[2] The article by Charles E. Brooks quotes from a small and lovely book by one "Kla-How-Ya" (a pen name) published in 1910. Kla-How-Ya describes his invention of a fabulously successful fly that he called simply the Pitcher, neglecting to mention its bipartite body. He began developing it in 1897 and worked on it for five years, which justifies the dating of its origin as 1902. He touted his new fly as the all-round best fly for Yellowstone Park, if not the entire mountain West.

And here I am, doting on it still. There was something national (as in Yellowstone National Park) about it after all. I'm amused to remember how hard it was for a boy to tie well and truly—at about four cents each—and I'm more than a little fond of recalling scrubbing those floors for old Ed and sneaking a peak over his shoulder as he tied slews of standard wet flies.

The Major Pitcher remains a handsome, elegant pattern with an interesting history. It deserves not to be forgotten utterly. I'd declare a centenary celebration of it if I could.

Still, trout flies, like old times, pass, and the centuries of our sport roll on. Let today's trout be content with their tiny, homelier, more realistic daily bread, rather than this lovely old fancy fly. It's flies like this that we can always enjoy collecting, tying, studying, and admiring, keeping their memory alive. They may not be art, but they suggest it. In any case, their fascination never wanes.

In Search of the Rio Grande King— and a Colorful Lady

No trout fly has figured more powerfully in the traditional Rocky Mountain angler's head and fly book than the Rio Grande King. George Leonard Herter, in his remarkable tackle-making manual of 1941, holds that the Rio Grande King was invented along with the Gunnison (an essentially forgotten pattern) by James Douglas of Denver, by my guess in the 1920s. How better to name a fly pattern than by the name of a great river.

Arthur H. Carhart, the father, one might argue, of the concept of national wilderness areas, and author of *Fishing in the West* (New York: Macmillan, 1950), notes that James Douglas is generally credited with the invention of the Rio Grande King. But, Carhart goes on, Douglas was associated with Englishman Bryan Haywood, who set up shop as a major commercial fly dresser in Denver in 1895. Carhart believed that Haywood, not Douglas, should be acknowledged as the creator of the great Rio Grande.

The original dressing called for a body of black ostrich herl along with the white duck-quill wing, brown hackle, and yellow tail. Herter calls for either ostrich herl or chenille for the body. Carhart states that a fat chenille body may not be as effective on the Rio Grande King as a thin, black silk body, which would be more realistic. To add to the confusion, a pattern identical to the Rio Grande with a narrow black silk body was commonly called the Captain in the mountain states. I recently found this antique Captain in an old, out-of-the-way general store in Utah where flies had accumulated unsold over the decades.

The Rio Grande King

But the interesting thing is that the reputation of Bryan Haywood, of early Denver fly-tying fame, inspired a Whitney Tackle Company salesman by the name of Harold Allen to change his name to Jim Haywood. This Haywood, an illustrious 1940s Denver version of Lee Wulff, was all things to all fishermen—a great fly caster, developer of new tackle, salesman, and personality. He was charismatic, widely admired, and emulated. Haywood tackle products were produced and sold by Whitney Sporting Goods Company of Denver, which sponsored Jim as its house pro.

Also, Carhart tells us, Bryan Haywood developed a famous western pattern called the Gunnison Special (not to be confused with the Gunnison mentioned earlier). This pattern had a pink body, brown hackle, and barred teal flank wing. Carhart tells how a Colorado angler took Gunnison Specials back East and had them copied by the important Weber Lifelike Fly Company of Steven's Point, Wisconsin. Somehow, Weber substituted a mallard-quill wing (gray) for the barred teal and called the fly Pink Lady. And so, out of a fairly obscure truly western pattern, a famous national one was born—according to Carhart.

Herter, and nearly everybody else, says to the contrary that the Pink Lady was the invention of the influential George LaBranche of New York, author, pioneer of the dry fly, and superb technician with a fly rod. Still, there is Carhart, with his claim that Colorado is the ultimate origin of the famous lady of the lovely pink body.

Which is to say that it becomes increasingly evident that Denver has a rich fly-fishing legacy, boasting colorful personalities and innovative tackle. Goodwin Granger's legendary cane rods, along with those of Bill Phillipson, both of Denver, now command high prices among collectors.

Not so grand a claim, perhaps, is that Denver is the site of the first closed-spool-type spinning reels, which were to sweep the nation.

Meanwhile, we ought not to forget pioneer and visionary Arthur Carhart's contribution to fly fishing and the earliest of environmental efforts in the West. He is seriously neglected. And what one wouldn't give to know more about Bryan Haywood and James Douglas, maybe even locate a date for the origin of the Rio Grande King.

The Question of the Royal Coachman

One of the most persistent questions about fly fishing is why the Royal Coachman catches fish when it resembles nothing in the world of insects. Perhaps this warrants a more careful response than it usually receives.

It's a fact that most of our established fly patterns have no specific counterpart in nature. The "realistic" dressings in which we specialize today, dressings that we think resemble real insects, are relatively new and few. Alternatively, we daily depend on a whole slew of modern attractor flies, some of them downright spectacular. And that's not to mention the myriad old fancy flies, of which the Royal Coachman is only, perhaps, the foremost representative. These fancy flies (have a look at the color plates in Ray Bergman's *Trout* or the new, huge, and stunning *Forgotten Flies* by Paul Schmookler and Ingrid Sils)[3] dominated the sport for most of two centuries. Their efficiency as fish takers doubtless had something to do with the willingness of our native brook trout to take almost any brightly colored fly. On the other hand, how can we be sure that a Royal Coachman, in its many variations, resembles nothing in nature to the trout. Perhaps it's richly suggestive of many good things to eat.

What is perhaps most essential to the effectiveness of the Royal Coachman is its body of peacock herl, maybe the single most effective material that can be employed in a trout fly, especially when combined with a brown hackle. Experienced fly fishermen know how effective any combination of brown and peacock is in any fly.

Then, too, we know that red, that most powerful of colors, is attractive to trout in countless fly dressings and so is aptly used for that central segment of the Royal's body.

Its modern tail of golden or amherst pheasant tippets (the original of 1878 had even gayer black-and-white-tipped lemon-duck flank fibers for tails) may suggest a trailing shuck. In fact, one wonders if all the fanciful tails of all our traditional flies do not, after all, suggest trailing shucks more than setae.

We should remember the old reliable Brown Hackle dressing, mainstay of fly books back in the nineteenth century, calling only for a simple peacock herl body and fiery brown hackle. Add but a white wing to this Brown Hackle, and suddenly we have the Coachman of distinguished English origin and history.

When in 1878, New Yorker John Haily added that segment of red floss midships of the peacock herl body, there was born our famous Royal Coachman—an American fly, but given its Anglophilic name by L. C. Orvis, brother of company founder Charles F. Orvis. That bit of sparkle, in this case from the red body segment, never hurt any fly, a fact we understand quite well today in our tying with all manner of sparkly material.

It remains only to comment on that highly visible white duck wing, the Royal Coachman's banner. We know that any fly that the angler can easily see will take more fish for him day in and day out. And so that banner is highly practical. But what of that same wing on a wet fly? Well, when wet-fly wings get beaten up, chewed up, and worn down, as they are wont to do, the fly only becomes more effective. Still, we wonder . . . those "unnatural" duck-quill wings on wets may be the very reason we no longer use them much.

There was a fabulous old Boulder fisherman who walked up Boulder Canyon and took many, many fish, and regularly.

His favorite pattern was the poor-man's western answer to the Royal Coachman, the Rio Grande King—just like the Royal in all but body, which had become simple black chenille, yet another pattern like nothing in nature. Our Boulder Creek master always chewed the white wing of his new wet Rio Grande down to a little white nub and killed fish right and left. His chewed-up King may well have been precisely what we now call an emerger.

The Royal Coachman

Finally, what with the great reputation and elegance of the Royal Coachman, along with its several virtues, the pattern becomes an article of faith, the faith necessary in any fly if it is to produce for us. The Royal Coachman may even be an impressionistic suggestion of a natural fly after all—and one that we can easily see in the water, to boot.

The Tups Indispensable
A Dubbing Dilemma

Somewhere at this moment, some nameless but responsible fly tier of good conscience is fretting over the near impossibility of finding exactly the correct dubbing for the thorax of a Tups Indispensable dry fly or nymph.

In the face of this fly's compelling lore, many of us fret over its dressing. In that fount of all knowledge, *The Oxford English Dictionary,* we learn that *tup* is cant for a ram or male sheep, and that the verb *to tup* denotes his dastardly act of covering (compelling) a gentle and innocent ewe. In Shakespeare's *Othello,* for example, the villain Iago seeks to poison Desdemona's father's mind against Othello by telling him that "an old black ram is tupping your white ewe."

In fly tying, *tups* refers to a delicate blend, an elusive shade and shine of dubbing based on a peculiar tint of urine-stained wool from the genitals of an old ram. Few fly tiers, if any, have seen the real thing. Resorting to frustrating guesswork, tiers have for a century sought to mix a dubbing that will satisfy for a Tups Indispensable fly, dry or nymph. The texts tell us to blend claret (or pink) and yellow wool or fur to simulate the desired shade. Some stipulate cream rather than yellow. All agree that it must be a delicate, subtle tint.[4]

But there is no visual standard by which to judge our blends. The Tups dressing is not widely available in shops. And if it were, what tier would dare to claim authority? Who is there to boast of having approached an old ram close enough for examination, let alone invited him to give up a sample? Of course, if we could find such a weathered old beast, and they are few, we could wait around for him simply to die or go to mutton, and then, in the spirit of the infamous Iago, snatch at his privates. But that surely speaks of a meanness of spirit and imagination.

So, we go on guessing, hunting materials, clipping, mixing, blending, and stirring about, in order to tie this lovely and useful dry fly or nymph correctly. Here on my desk lies a small packet of dyed "tups" wool from the redoubtable John Veniard's of London, dated 1965. It is pinker than some would think correct, but then who are we to argue with John Veniard? He speaks with an authority as close to the great tradition and to the pasture as we shall get.

G.E.M. Skues, England's heroic father of the nymph, was the first to use the Tups in 1900—and with stunning success, he himself "dubbing" it "Indispensable." He kept the complex formula of the dub[5] a deep secret for several years before revealing it as too important to deny to other anglers.

The Tups Nymph was also a major player in James E. Leisenring's fly book. He tells us how to tie it in his great *The Art of Tying the Wet Fly* (New York: Dodd, Mead, 1941). We know that Leisenring enjoyed an extensive and important correspondence with Skues, that they exchanged flies across the Atlantic, and that each much admired the other. We may fairly suspect that Big Jim got his enthusiasm for the Tups from Skues and then made it his own basic American nymph.

The fly appears here and there in the pattern books, with optional bodily proportions. More common to the dry fly, we see a tag of primrose yellow floss and a regular body of tups dubbing. The nymph, however, ought to be tied with a yellow floss abdomen and a pronounced bump of a thorax of tups dubbing just behind the hackle. We are told that the fly, both dry and nymph, may be tied with either a pale honey dun or equally pale blue dun hackle. Hackle for the nymph must be soft, quite short, and sparse. The dry is, of course, wingless.

Leisenring calls for two of the tiniest dun hackle points for tails on the nymph. They ought to extend beyond the bend of the hook by no more than an eighth of an inch on a size 14 dressing. Tails for the dry are the more conventional bunched matching hackle barbules. Yellow tying silk, giving the fly a dull yellow head, is preferred. As, of course, is the correct dubbing.

Christmas Silk

I must have been fourteen that day,
With my first silk line in the air.
Its energy flowing smooth and supple,
Loading and unloading,
Like a willow full of wind,
Over lower Boulder Creek.

The amber silk bore my flies
To trout I hardly dared to think
Could be there just for me—
Those rainbows slashing
At my Rio Grande King.

Something worked for me that day.
That silk in the air had done it.
That first time:
The tug of Life in the air.[6]

When, now and then, the conversation turns to fly lines,
I often claim to my skeptical friends that my right
arm still remembers the feel of casting the old
oil-processed silk lines: that ineffable pull as the
backcast straightens "the tug of Life in the air."

Even though silk lines disappeared in about
1945 in favor of our admirable and efficient modern plastics, I can now test that claim to muscle
memory, because Englishman Noel Buxton has
recovered the technology of the vacuum-pro-
cessed silk fly lines in the great tradition of P. D.
Malloch's "Kingfisher" lines that for so long set
the standard. Buxton has for the last few years
offered his lines to the trade under the brand

name Phoenix, if for the highly significant figure of about $2 per foot—a less alarming way of naming the price but understandable when one realizes how labor-intensive their manufacture is. (My first silk line, a seventy-five-foot level size E, Weber Henshall, cost my parents a whopping $2.50 in 1939.)

So I agonized and then decided that I'd mortgage the farm and buy one of these new old silk lines as a Christmas present to myself. My mental balance became even more questionable to my friends when I declared that, by God, I came to fishing the fly in 1939 throwing silk, so I might as well go out throwing it—at least on special occasions. They only shook their heads and walked away.

It was both difficult and exciting to wait for Christmas morning just like a little kid to see the wondrous new line. But I managed. It was worth it.

As companion tackle to the silk line, I've got vintage 1948 five-strip cane rods, old Hardy reels, and even a couple—three dozen English drawn silkworm gut leaders—too tedious and difficult really to use, even for me, a certified, if not certifiable, troglodytic Luddite—a mouthful of vocabulary, I know, but a precise admission of an old man's effort to preserve the pleasures and satisfactions of his past.

My new DT 5 Christmas silk lies here before me as I write, brand-new and simply boxed, in its tight golden coil, with all the fragrance of the oils of its impregnation and finish rising from it. It's lovely stuff begging to be cast.

Because it's significantly smaller in diameter, it's therefore less wind-resistant than the modern plastics, and because it has no stretch, it feels different in the air, more dynamic and positive. It seems to concentrate and control energy more efficiently.

A fundamental difference between silk and plastic is that the silk line's casting weight is in the core of properly tapered braided silk. The modern plastic-coated Dacron lines get their weight from the thickness of the plastic coating over a very thin Dacron center.

Important to the manufacture of these silk lines (in the 1870s in the United States, some historians maintain) was the vacuum process in which raw braided lines are placed in a vacuum chamber along with oils, largely linseed and tung, and the air pumped out. This vacuum process draws the oils thoroughly into the braided silk. Then, on the surface, successive coats of oil are applied, cured, and hand rubbed until the last coating, called the "varnish," is applied, cured, and finally honed again.

The disadvantage of all this is that these lines need considerable care. They must be dried after each use in order to discourage the rot that can attack any organic substance. And they must never suffer prolonged, severe heat at the risk of making the oils run, leaving the line hopelessly tacky. Then, too, only by greasing the lines at least daily will they float really well. The careful old-timers, when they got home, always took their lines off the reel, dressed them, and hung them in loose coils until the next trip. With such care, a silk would last as long and float as well as the plastics of today.

I'm counting on that in order for me and this line to get through the next few years I'll have on the stream—if I'm lucky.

Anyhow, it was a wonderful Christmas present in 1939, and it feels almost as good again now. If, when I get this line on my little Hardy LRH reel and toss my flies into Boulder Creek, my arm should fail the test of its memory, I'll never admit it. After all, I'm invested in my past.

Flinging Spinners

Come to think of it, we did awful things with our fly rods back in those days when we didn't know any better, before this golden age of fly fishing began. We lobbed worms, we swam minnows, we chucked lures, and we flung spinners off the tips of our fly rods. We even cast flies.

For better or worse, our fly rods were all-purpose tools, butted up with that emblem of the western angler: the automatic reel. Our oil-processed silk lines may or may not have been the right size for our particular rods. Precision was difficult to achieve, as line size was determined according to line diameter, not by weight as they are today. Most of us just "felt" a rod—wiggled it a bit, and, right or wrong, sensed a line size, probably a D or C, on the heavy side of 5 or 6 AFTM. A heavy level gut leader of three to six feet with a dropper loop constituted the terminal tackle. Few blood knots ever had to be tied.

But there was one thing we could do with this rig, and that was to fling fly-rod spinners around all up and down our streams. The interbellum period was the great age of the fly-rod spinner, and no trout fisherman worthy of his rod would be caught on the water without a few of these distinctly American lures. We fished them mostly in streams where the currents helped to spin and wobble them into that tantalizing appeal that brought the trout to an abandoned, slashing, angry, often visible strike. It was really great fun, except in still water where working the spinner blades was difficult and often frustrating.

The Spinners Themselves:

the Colorado, the Indiana, the Willow Leaf,
the Areoplane, the Bear Valley, the June Bug

In brass, copper, and nickel.

Colorado spinners

The Colorado was basic. (I wonder how it got its name?) Its blade spun on a split ring between two swivels and was usually fished with bare ice-tong hooks. But the Indiana, with a slightly elongated, more spoon-shaped blade, was mounted by a clevice turning on a wire shaft and was more often than not fished with a cheap hackle fly or trailing worm. The Willow Leaf was, as the name suggests, long and narrow of blade and would spin very fast indeed. The stores were full of Denver-made Areoplane spinners—a great favorite—which featured a propeller blade and red beads. But I remember how pretty I thought the Bear Valley spinner, with its red glass beads and hammered copper blade of Colorado spinner shape. Least popular was the June Bug, rather Midwestern, and proper to those big pike and muskie rigs of Pflueger specialty.

And then there were the fly rod "lures" such as the Southbend Trix Oreno, the Pflueger Chum, miniature Dardevles, or the famous Helin Flatfish. They were heavier and more awkward to fish, but lest we worry overmuch about that, I'm sure that all of us today from time to time cast big weighted nymphs every bit as heavy and dangerous to the back of the head.

I remember, too, how exciting it was to send off a dime in reply to the little half-inch ads in *Field and Stream* that offered the latest bright idea in spinners. Invention was endless. Hildebrandt of Indiana was (and still is) the great name in the industry.

One spinner made its way to Boulder around 1943. E. B. Edwards, my mentor, of local tackle/jewelry-shop fame and dean of Boulder's fly-rod spinner men, discovered the Nova Spinner and sold a slew of them. The Nova had an ultralight metal blade, a half-propeller, that spun in-line on a wire shaft. Held downstream in the current, it would spin so fast as to disappear in a blur, but cast well upstream and drifted and flirted back down, it was deadly. Ed insisted that this Nova wanted size 18 or 20 treble hooks held in the spinner's wire snap. He was able to supply these tiny trebles, the likes of which none of us had seen before.

Anyway, the Nova worked wonders. It cast like a dream and was lovely, delicate fishing in clear, medium-to-low creeks. The ultimate, as far as I was concerned back then. Now as I write, a single remaining Nova hangs here, in memoriam, in front of me.

Of course, it was the advent of the spinning reel that spelled doom for the fly-rod spinner. With the fixed-spool reel we could toss little hunks of metal down to a sixteenth of an ounce great distances. And who can remember without embarrassment the way this revolutionary technique and tackle killed fish in those immediate postwar years?

In any case, those special little fly-rod spinners have all but disappeared. Something lost, almost forgotten, but here remembered. I think that I shall take my last little Nova up Boulder Creek this spring, toss it upstream, and flirt it in the face of a certain rainbow willing to conspire with me in a ceremony of recollection. I even have the size 20 treble hook left over from so long ago.

Fly Fishing and World War Two
Retreat, Advance, and Democracy

The Second World War violently interrupted and profoundly changed the course of American fly fishing. Three generations of fly fishermen put away their tackle for the duration and went off to war. In Europe, the South Pacific, and at sea, angler soldiers and sailors had somehow to sustain themselves with dreams of home and fly rod. No one can know how many of those rods were put aside forever.

Those who returned as veterans in 1945, the war over at last, found nearly everything about their old, prewar lives changing fast. The fly fishing that they had left behind, traditional and rather limited, was on the brink of explosive development and a democratization of the sport that would allow it to grow, after the compromising advent of spinning, into the greatly popular phenomenon it is today.

The vets came home to find cane rods glued up with new war-industry-developed marine glues that were impervious to almost everything. No longer need they fear that the bamboo strips of a rod might at any time sweat loose. Nylon was set to replace silk in their lines, and perhaps most important of all, nylon monofilament would transform their leaders. The new nylon terminal tackle—efficient, inexpensive, durable, and not in need of constant attention—would be a great new democratizer of fly fishing, to say nothing of providing fine-diameter tippets suitable for flies much smaller than were ever practical before. Nylon was the touchstone of fly fishing's popularity to come. Anyone and everyone could now fish the fly.

At the same time, the development of limp nylon in hundred-yard spools made practical the use of the European spinning (fixed-spool) reel. The French sent over spools of the best stuff, of which .008-inch diameter tested a full three pounds. It was a revelation.

Before nylon monofilament, all manner of material had been used with less than success for lines on the fixed-spool reel, which had lain doggo in Europe as though waiting only for postwar nylon to appear. Quite suddenly, spinning reels, for what the English called "threadline fishing," came to the United States from England, France, Italy, and Switzerland and got the revolution going full blast. The French Luxor arrived on these shores, accompanied by the likes of the Swiss Fix, the Hardy, and the Young Beaudex—all the open-faced "coffee grinders." American entrepreneur Bache Brown would take the Luxor and make it a U.S. citizen, calling it the Airex and later the Master Reel. The Mitchell came from France, and so it went. The market boomed. This upstart spinning tackle and its technique would seriously dislocate and distract countless anglers from their fly fishing.

The United States moved quickly for its share of the new market by producing the enclosed-spool-type spinning reel. The I. V. Humphrey reel, the stainless-steel "tin can" from Denver, was the first of this kind that would prove popular for the less demanding angling public.

At first there were no lures specifically for spinning. Pioneer spinning fishermen had to fall back on the heavier bait-casting spoons, spinners, and plugs in their bass tackle boxes. Most of a year passed before the European lures appeared, followed hard upon by Bache Brown's American models. The metal lure market exploded in turn with every variety of hardware imaginable.

The spinning boom appeared to bury fly fishing. Few could resist the new enthusiasm. Certainly trout could not. They fell readily, even greedily, to the hardware thrown amazing distances to them. Any angler, after fifteen minutes of instruction, could master the fixed-spool reel and cast a quarter-ounce wobbler 150 feet. With small lures on the new light lines so effective, why bother with that difficult old fly tackle?

Many of those who had fished the fly before the war were quickly seduced by spinning. The new generation that had neither fished flies nor been to war were pushovers for spinning. Many, when they had thoughts of flies, merely tied on a plastic ball or "bubble," partly filled with water for weight, attached four or five feet of monofilament and any old fly, and spun this rig a hundred feet cast after cast, covering a vast expanse of water. Stocked trout especially simply could not resist.

What, then, came to the rescue of fly fishing? What was it that restored fly fishermen to their senses and their flies? Several things happened. Highly efficient, inexpensive, durable new fly rods of fiberglass cloth appeared, making casting the fly easier and less arcane. These new rods were part of the same wave of democratization that nylon terminal tackle had begun. Also, to the delight of those who wanted to be expert, the development in San Francisco of the shooting-head fly line (thirty feet of fly line attached to 100 yards or so of monofilament shooting line) came as a revelation. Suddenly a fly fisher could throw a fly nearly as far as a spin fisherman could his quarter-ounce lure. Everybody seemed to want to realize Charles Cotton's ancient advice in Walton's *Compleat Angler:* to fish "fine and far off."

Then, too, there was sudden development in flies, fly tying, and general at-home tackle making. The influence of George Leonard Herter and his company in Waseca, Minnesota, on this was immense. Herter's supplied an inclusive line of fly-tying materials, rod, and general tackle-making supplies. It is fair to say that Herter's demystified both the definition and the supply of all the materials a serious angler needed. The famous Herter's catalog read like an encyclopedia—not without the chuckles that the eccentric George Herter's descriptive style elicited. In any case, Herter's was an important extension of the steady democratization of postwar fly fishing.

In the West a new genre of attractor fly dressings for big water were exciting to tie and to fish. In the East, innovative angling theorists like Vincent Marinaro and Charles Fox were opening up a new world of terrestrial-insect representation for trout. With the new light terminal tackle, these flies took fish almost as fast as hardware.

One writer, perhaps more than the rest, summoned his readers to fly fishing's new day. A. J. McClane's columns in *Field and Stream* discussed fly fishing with a new sophistication and technical detail more than adequate to satisfy the most demanding angler, especially the new, young, ambitious angler who, as often as not, suffered an unrelieved craving for new angling lore and technology. To satisfy this craving, serious and innovative fly tackle and techniques became widely available to all. The old tempter spinning began to seem too simple, too easy, no longer as satisfying as it once was. And by the close of the fifties, trout had begun to wise up. They were no longer duped by just any old wobbler hurled out there a country mile and dragged back past them time after time.

The revival of many a lapsed fly fisher came with the discovery that while a given trout could now watch a spoon wobble by any number of times and turn away in boredom, a size 22 fur ant could make the same fish jump through the hoops of the fly angler's technique and into his net.

Not to be overlooked was the rapid development of transportation and its crucial importance to the expansion of fishing of all kinds. Interstate highways, better automobiles, and airlines made possible the modern version of the old American Dream of going anywhere, anytime—the democracy of the road.

So, between 1945 and 1955, angling culture was not only restored, but greatly enhanced and democratized. The foundation was laid for what would be the immense and surprising burst of popularity of fly fishing in the 1980s, when it became fashionable—almost a craze—among the Boomer population. But that's another story.

Stories About It

A Memoir of Trout and Eros
Following L. B. France Into Colorado's Middle Park

L. B. France, an early Denver attorney, was the first important writer on trout fishing in Colorado. With wit and grace he sang its praises and did much to spread the good news eastward, helping draw myriad anglers to the western wildernesses.

Reading France's *With Rod and Line in Colorado Waters* (1884),[7] and his accounts of his fishing forays more than a century ago into Middle Park on Colorado's Western Slope, I recalled again my own foray to the tiny Middle Park town of Fraser in the summer of 1940. My pharmacist uncle and aunt, Les and Irmogene Murrin, were operating the Fraser drug and general store and invited me to spend a week with them fishing the Fraser valley's subalpine and still pristine waters. Now, moved by reading France, I see that this was my first real, honest-to-God, away-from-home fishing trip—a heady experience for a boy of fourteen obsessed with trout and the tackle to catch them.

And I recall how this first big fishing trip had about it another dimension, an event of seminal power enough to change a boy into an new creature, one suddenly faced with the anguish of growing up. Now, through the lenses of that pioneer Colorado angler of long ago, I can see and feel that week of mine in all the richness and heartbreak of refreshed memory. It began like this.

The Trout

One weekend, my father and mother drove me from Boulder over Berthoud Pass and down into Fraser, planning to return for me a week later. It was a long, tough drive in those days. My expectation of great fishing made the trip take forever, or so it seemed, but Mother's cold fried chicken helped make it bearable. But at last we were coasting easily down that long, straight canyon corridor, past West Portal into Middle Park and on to Fraser. Streams of living water seemed to flow everywhere, along the canyon floor and out into the Park, onto the vast and beautiful prairies of superb wild hay. I was out of my head with excitement: each little run of water through the grass, I thought, must surely be full of hungry, eager trout. Trout, all was trout, the possibility of trout everywhere. I was a boy besotted; all the elements of air and earth sang to me of trout.

Those enchanted, lush, and limitless meadows of Middle Park had to have been much as France had known them sixty years earlier, only now they were the stomping ground of lumbering and ranching Swedes, and workers on the Denver and Salt Lake Railroad, which bisected the Park on its way down to Utah.

Anyhow, we soon pulled off the main road and into Fraser—a few unadorned, white clapboard buildings set down seemingly at random on equally few acres. One of them was a rickety two stories tall, and most were fronted with low, uncovered plank porches. Fraser had no discernible walkways, certainly nothing like a main street, only the irregular dirt spaces between buildings, dusty when dry and muddy when wet. Everything man-made seemed to have sprung up at random or been dumped there arbitrarily. Around the small core of buildings, here and there out in the meadows, were low-lying rough log cabins, lean-tos, little corrals, sheds, ricks of lumber and hay, a barn or two, wagons in various states of repair, and a few livestock. The entire scene was hushed and still, nothing moving, caressingly cool, moist and yet dry, sun-drenched, intensely blue of sky, every kind of green in the yellow-flowered meadows, lonesome white buildings, more lonesome yet the outlying cabins—the entire prospect contained in a vessel of crystalline, intoxicating air.

Right there in the center of town stood the Fraser Drug, only slightly more imposing, as I remember, than the other buildings, with its old, roughly painted sign over the door. It was my Uncle Les and Aunt Irmogene's enterprise, boasting a soda fountain and, to galvanize my consciousness, a small counter full of fishing tackle.

Attached to the drugstore on the south side were rough but cosy living quarters, entered just behind the soda fountain, near the fishing tackle. Never before had I enjoyed free access to that much tackle to study and memorize—those boxes of snelled wet flies; two or three dozen dry flies; three or four automatic fly reels; assorted leaders, some of them tapered; packets of snelled hooks; sinkers; and the obligatory cards of spinners: Colorado, Bear Valley, and Areoplane. The purest of fly fishermen would not be without a couple of spinners, just in case. There were the necessary creels for a legal limit of twenty-five trout and, of course, half a dozen nine-foot bamboo fly rods on a rack nearby, rods that today we have learned to call "production grade," priced at around $12 to $20. Also a few pairs of hip boots. I hesitate to think how much time I spent poring over and handling this stock of tackle, in terrible rushes of angling fantasy.

The first two days, my uncle and aunt took me to some fishing on small streams around Fraser, fishing that didn't amount to much. Accustomed to the freestone creeks of the Colorado Front Range, I hardly knew how to handle those meandering but fast willow-bound, high meadow streams. My flies and spinners just didn't work. Probably my flies were too big, coarse, and ill chosen (I had no entomology at all). My presentation would have been clunky and ruined by drag—sufficient to keep me fishless in any such paradise.

I remember, after those disappointments, deciding to take my angling fortunes into my own hands. Next day, I would simply strike out, walking the highway south, half a mile out of town, to a little dirt track that took off from the highway and into the meadow, and after a few hundred yards met the Fraser River itself. There I would fish to my heart's content, and just maybe accomplish something.

But the Fraser was just like the other creeks I'd been fishing, only bigger. At first there were the same frustrations and failures. But things were about to change.

I can't remember exactly why I did what I did next, but I sat down in the deep grass in the willows and cut the Red Variant dressing from the small dry-fly hook bent to the tapered gut leader. With the same knife I dug into the black, wet earth for a worm. And found one. It must have been from sheerest economy that I decided to fish no more than half an inch of that worm at a time. Impaling it on the little, light wire hook, with no sinker, I tossed it straight up the current ahead of me, close to the overhanging bank, out from under which came this trout that took my little hunk of worm as though it were a fly. It was a wonderful fight. And it was a wonderful brook trout of more than a pound.

Maybe there had never been so beautiful a fish, such a prize. With him in the net, I calmed down a little, observed all rightful ceremony, and got him into my creel. Up and at 'em again, but still dazzled, I sent forth, up the Fraser, yet another small piece of worm with the same result, only this time a slightly smaller brookie, as jewel-like and vibrant as the first.

And so it went, dependent only on my finding another worm or two to divide among those willing trout. Such hard fighters they were in that heavy, deep water—the water that brook trout like best. Fishing that tiny bit of worm on a fly hook and finely tapered leader directly upstream and close to the bank, allowing it to drift down as freely as possible in the surface, brought those trout up out of the depths with utter abandon. I was in triumph. Two of my fish would go two pounds. What a fine mess of trout! There'd been nothing like it in my life before.

But then there arose the sudden fear that I'd gone over the legal weight limit of ten pounds and one fish. So, though not overly worried about meeting a game warden, and not too troubled of conscience, I stopped at thirteen, all brook trout, a memorable catch if ever there was one.

As I walked back up the narrow cow path to the highway, those thirteen fish, which would weigh in at fifteen pounds gutted, were a serious burden in the creel on my shoulder. So, wanting to show off this catch, wanting the world—at least everyone in Middle Park—to know what I'd accomplished, I threaded the fish onto a sturdy willow fork and set off on the half mile back to Fraser and the drugstore, where I would surely be received in triumph. The few cars and trucks that came down that old highway, I made sure got an eyeful of my fish. I probably swaggered shamelessly.

Back at the store, I was indeed received with high praise. The fish went to the refrigerator, awaiting the ride back to Boulder, and I headed for the soda fountain. Talk about satisfaction.

Anyhow, I could now coast along for the remainder of my Middle Park week, rest on my laurels, and go home to Boulder in glory. I stayed close to the soda fountain and that tackle counter and felt like an expert full of useful advice for any tourist who might stop in to ask about the local trouting. I was quite certain I'd struck upon a great new light-tackle technique for taking trout with my fragment of worm fished like a fly.

But the euphoria wasn't to last. I was in for a fall. It happened like this.

Eros [8]

Uncle Les and Aunt Irmogene were given now and then to enjoy a few drinks at bar-and-grills, roadhouses with dance halls that they found agreeable. So, when my parents arrived on Saturday to fetch me home on Sunday, Uncle and Aunt urged Mother and Dad to go with them that night down to

Granby to a joint they liked that had a good dance band. And it would be perfectly all right for me to come along, there being, in those days, no prejudice against children in such places. Besides, I'd be protected by doting family.

So off we went that evening, down the Fraser valley to where that river meets the great Colorado at Granby. I was still awash in self-satisfaction from my day on the river and eager for this new, grown-up experience.

The roadhouse bar-and-grill, a rustic pine-log affair, was big enough inside for a few tables, booths, a small bandstand, dance floor, and bar swagged in colored lights. An aromatic amalgam of stale beer, tobacco, and hamburgers pervaded the dimly lit room. I'd never been in such a place. It felt faintly illicit, even dangerous. That it was nearly empty made it seem even more so.

The adults ordered highballs and I got a bottle of pop. The dance band arrived—men of uncertain, well-used, dour middle age—and began almost grudgingly to play the popular swing numbers of the day. It was all very agreeable: Percy, Thelma, Irmogene, and Les relaxing to the measure of the music and the whiskey, dancing, enjoying themselves in a way I'd not seen with my parents before. They were absorbed, caught up in a secret, sensual world all their own, forbidden, I realized with some alarm, for me to enter.

Just then, more people came in—a family of three—and took a booth just beyond us, fully in my view. A mother, a father, and a daughter, just about my age, who now sat facing me across maybe twenty feet of charged space. She sat there in the palpable obscurity of the room in a halo of her own light. Our eyes met, and I was altogether hers.

Though I should never in the world back then have understood the words I now attribute to her, she was, nevertheless, exquisitely Pre-Raphaelite in her loveliness.

My mouth dried up on my Orange Crush, my stomach turned over. I felt shaky and must have stared outrageously. And she stared back with a solemn, unblinking candor that undid me. The grown-ups knew at once what was going on and began teasing me a little, Aunt Irmogene egging me on to go ask the girl to dance. Me? Ask her to dance? Me, with my junior-high-gymnasium dance steps? The prospect was terrifying.

It must have taken a full half hour of persuasion for me to get up the courage to do it—in a public dance hall, to go ask a beautiful girl to dance. But it had to be done—I guessed.

I was shaking in my timbers as I crossed the great gulf of those twenty feet to their booth, looking first at her unresponsive parents and only then at her. "Would you like to dance?"

"No, thank you."

I heard it as though from far, far away as my world crashed down around me. I felt so ashamed, so certain that I'd done something terrible and had been told, in fact, that there was something absolutely and forever wrong with me—an indictment that proved indelible.

Somehow, I got back to the bosom of my family, but the rest of the evening was significantly muted and for me full of self-doubt and heartache—just the opposite of my midweek elation and sense of accomplishment on the river.

My grown-ups understood what had happened and treated me carefully, even lovingly, but I suspect that down deep they were amused at this moment in the human comedy played out in front of them. They probably had been there before me.

Riding in silence back through the deep mountain night to Fraser, I tried to call up the thrill and happiness of those brook trout, but ever and again the countenance of that girl rose up to fill me with longing and misery. I was still caught in her gaze, that gaze of yearning and gentle sorrow, utterly still and changeless, dreaming. And I had thought that there might be a place in that dreaming for me. If only I could have caught those fish for her.

Next day with my parents, and like L. B. France before me, I would recross the Continental Divide back over

Berthoud Pass to the realities of home and growing up, leaving Middle Park behind as a sort of
abiding mythology of adventure, the crossing of
a divide in the heart of a boy "which hurts and is
desired."

Now, so many years later, I cannot be certain
whether it was that girl who broke the heart I
offered her that summer night or the fine mess of
brook trout that I treasure most in memory. But I
am sure that those trout, which rose to a piece of
worm as to a fly, were a solid accomplishment.

Bringing Back the Greenback

Oncorhynchus clarki stomias, the greenback cutthroat trout, native to the watersheds of
Colorado's South Platte and Arkansas River
systems.

The cutthroat trout has become the glamour fish
of the Mountain West. In Colorado, the particularly beautiful and native greenback variety, rediscovered and saved from extinction, is the most

glamorous of them all. How this lovely and delicate fish was rescued after being thought extinct for so long is a tale of two cultures—first, of the early 1950s, then of the late 1960s.

In 1952, University of Colorado graduate student and angler Bill Rickard felt sure he had found greenback cutthroat in a tiny creek up on the side of the Continental Divide west of Boulder. His discovery went unpublished and unheralded. Even had it been, who would have cared?

Anglers back then held the cutthroat in little esteem. Though well regarded on the table, it was considered a poor fighter and rather too easy, too uninteresting, to pursue. Indeed, the ease of its capture is in part responsible for its decline. Anyhow, rainbows and browns better suited the established idea of what a trout ought to be. Furthermore, raising cutthroat in hatcheries was difficult and expensive, the practice neglected. The carefully protected Yellowstone blackspotted cutthroat in its native Yellowstone Lake and River was the exception. It was and is eagerly fished, not for its species, but rather for its numbers and good average size.

The long and short of the matter is that in 1952, when that young Colorado scientist got excited by some small trout he caught and came to suspect they were native greenbacks, few anglers felt any particular interest in "natives" or any investment in the idea of "nativism" as activists promote it today. And even if that first and early rediscovery of the greenback had been well publicized and promoted, it is still highly doubtful that there would have been the enthusiasm necessary to re-establish secure and fishable populations of this old Rocky Mountain speckled trout.

But times change. Seventeen years later, in 1969, amid social revolution, the greenback was officially rediscovered. Only after that date and its agonizing realignment of social, economic, and political sensibilities could anglers, ecologists, and politicians come to appreciate and support the ascendancy of a native species over the "exotics," as non-native species were beginning to be called.

The angling worm of those tumultuous times turned toward the New Left, nativism becoming the sign of the times on the environmental, ecological, and associated political fronts. No fish was better qualified than the Colorado greenback to lead the way to the restoration of conditions as nearly pre-European as possible, conditions in which native fishes could thrive in the Rocky Mountains. In 1994, the Colorado legislature nearly stampeded to proclaim the greenback the state fish, replacing, with a stroke of the pen, the tough, dependable, admirable rainbow, now ignominiously under suspicion as "that interloper from California."

If the first cutthroats evolved in the Pacific Northwest from the parent rainbow, one may well ask how they found their way to the interior Rockies, where they adapted so well and individually to various troutless watersheds like the Snake, the Colorado, the Rio Grande, the Platte, and the Yellowstone.[9] Students of salmonid development now feel quite sure that the mechanism for this movement was the sudden occurrence, in periods of glaciation, of ice dams (seismic events may have played a role, too) that blocked ordinarily westward-flowing streams on their way to the Pacific. These ice dams forced both water and trout back over the shoulders of the Rocky Mountains, even over the Continental Divide, to flow down south and east in streams old and new.

Lewis and Clark, on their momentous way west in 1804, were the first Europeans to describe the cutthroat as a species; William Clark was to have his name forever tied to all its varieties as *Oncorhynchus clarki*. The fish frequently stood between the company of explorers and the terrors of hunger.

Soon thereafter, westering mountain men, explorers, and pioneers making their way to the Rocky Mountains and beyond were to find and value this excellent food fish. Those who took the northerly route from the Missouri and the Platte into the Northwest found the varieties encountered by Lewis and Clark—those immediately related to the Pacific drainages. They were plentiful, delicious, and willing prey.

With the discovery of gold in Colorado in 1859, not a few of those restless new westerners, instead of taking the northern, Oregon route, turned south, following the South Platte River into the Colorado Territory, where, in the mountains west of what would become Denver, they found the Front Range streams filled with a beautiful "speckled" trout, again delicious and willing. This trout, almost surely a speciation from the Colorado River variety of cutthroat, made itself at home in the drainages of the South Platte and the more southerly Arkansas River of Colorado's Eastern Slope. The greenback was heavily fished, fair and foul, both for sport and as a valuable addition to the frontier diet.

All too soon—essentially by 1890—the greenback was nearly gone. Pollution from mining, deforestation, commercial fishing, unlimited sporting bag limits, and the fish's unfortunate vulnerability had done their dirty work.

Coincidentally, Rocky Mountain tourism was gearing up, with railroads playing a key role in that development. Realizing the importance of good fishing for tourists, the railroads, in cahoots with the federal government, were quick to stock the new and exciting rainbow from California into the fished-out waters of Colorado's Front Range. The rainbow seemed the answer to the trout fisherman's prayer, the cutthroat quickly and easily forgotten. The last authenticated greenback was recorded in 1906 by distinguished University of Colorado naturalist T.A.D. Cockerell.

For at least eighty years, Colorado Rocky Mountain anglers were to get along quite happily, fishing good populations of imported rainbows, browns, and brooks.

Then, in 1969, with cultural revolution everywhere, a new public consciousness about all things natural in place, the internationally distinguished salmonid scholar Dr. Robert Behnke, at Colorado State University at Fort Collins, announced that he and his associates had found a surviving population of the greenback cutthroat high in the mountains, only a few miles west of Boulder in a tiny run of water known as Como Creek, an extremely rugged tributary of North Boulder Creek. Como tumbles headlong right through the University of Colorado's Mountain Research Station. (This essay might as readily be thought of as a tale of two universities.) Como slows down here and there barely enough to allow a few small trout to hold on.

Professor Behnke, using the best scientific technologies, identified these little trout as the primeval greenback. Much was made of this good news, and plans for its recultivation were immediately put in place.

Behnke soon discovered yet another pure strain of this fish in the Little South Fork of the Cache la Poudre River, a more northerly feeder in the South Platte system. He also found a small but pure population to the south in a tributary of the Arkansas, and an elusive, genetically doubtful population in Rocky Mountain National Park in the headwaters of the Big Thompson River.

Though these national-park "greenbacks" themselves came to nothing, Rocky Mountain National Park proved an excellent fostering ground for the first new populations of greenbacks based on Como Creek and Poudre River brood stocks. Self-sustaining populations of these beautiful little trout quickly took hold there with the help, in 1973, of the Endangered Species Act. These fish did well enough that by 1978, the "endangered" classification could be eased to "threatened," and new waters remote from the dangers of other trout competition and hybridization, stocked with greenbacks. It has been a gratifying success story of more than twenty stable populations, now providing quite good no-kill greenback fly fishing.

But there remains the tale of the struggling University of Colorado graduate student embarking on serious, advanced research in biological sciences. Bill Rickard[10] had returned from World War II to begin work on an undergraduate degree in biology. An accomplished fly fisherman and promising scientist with the sensibility of a classical naturalist, he spent three summers of study at the alpine Science Lodge, as today's Mountain Research Station was then known.

Almost by accident, he noticed the small trout in Como Creek, which ran outside his cabin. As a lark, he caught a few and puzzled over them. They were obviously cutthroat, carrying that distinguishing slash of red just under the jaw, but otherwise were unlike any he had ever seen in his extensive Colorado fishing. As much scientist as angler, he began reading in the technical literature and soon came to suspect that he just might have found the long-gone greenback.

Rickard took specimens down to Boulder to the single professor in his university department who was interested in fishes. Said the professor, "Bill, you're wasting my time and your own. The greenback is extinct. Forget it." Nor would the professor accept any of Rickard's specimens.

By then it was too late for Bill to pursue his discovery to publication. He had to get on with his own quite different and demanding research on plants, down on his knees at the atomic test site in the Mojave Desert.

He bore up silently under the summary rejection of his alma mater and left Colorado and his bottled specimens of greenbacks on the dusty shelves of the Mountain Research Station. Robert Behnke and the men from Colorado State University, seventeen years later, following up on institutional memory and scientific rumor, went to Como Creek and found Rickard's bottles on the shelves and the fish in the creek. The rest, as they say, is history.

The cultural climate, in convulsions of change, had prepared the way with new dispensations in both society and science, allowing for full appreciation of this achievement. The times were now ready for bringing back this distinguished Colorado native, the greenback cutthroat.

An Essential Item of Tackle

In my callow youth, I nursed an obsessive need for more and more, better and better fishing tackle. After discharge from World War II in 1946, what with going off to college, I needed a car to get me and my girlfriend around town and into the mountains fishing. Cars were still scarce that soon after the war, but I was lucky enough to find a slick little 1937 Chevy coupe. Turned out that keeping it running was its own financial burden, one that got in the way of having ever more tackle. Though I daily fantasized about new rods and reels, eventually I came to my senses and realized that my little car was, in fact, my most essential piece of fishing tackle. After all, it got me where I needed to go to fish.

I tried to be satisfied.

Girlfriend Betty became fiancée, and then wife in June 1948. Off on a three-week honeymoon to Yellowstone country, we hoped to fish about fifteen of those twenty-one days. (Betty had taken up the fly rod during our engagement and caught on fast.) We left our Denver hotel early, striking out for Cheyenne and points north, hoping to make it maybe as far as the Big Horn Basin before dark. We were driving that valued piece of fishing tackle, that dear old black Chevy coupe, itself eleven years old already.

We passed Cheyenne before noon. On north, though the road was paved all the way, it was nevertheless barely two lanes wide and hugged

For the first time, the very newest
things in motor car beauty, comfort,
safety and performance come to you
with the additional advantage of being
thoroughly proved, thoroughly reliable.

the contours of the rolling high plains intimately. We drove
around every knoll, down into and up out of every little draw
and gully. We were certain that the road was following old
trails and stage routes (there were no interstates back then).
But all was well—we were happy, full of life, and driving
along nicely. Until.

About ninety miles north of Cheyenne, an ugly noise
began coming from the engine. Out there in those vast and
empty Wyoming spaces, we were scared and sickened by what
we heard. There was nothing to do but keep going, in hopes
of reaching Glendo, maybe fifteen miles ahead, before the
car broke down completely.

The noise got steadily worse, our apprehension along with it. The Chevy's engine was obviously trying to throw a connecting rod. There's not a worse sound in all of nature. I know that philosopher of music John Cage claimed to hear musical value in any sound, but I'll wager he never had to listen to a connecting rod trying to hammer its way out of an engine block out in the emptiness of the Wyoming prairies.

I'll never forget what a relief it was to see the tiny town of Glendo appear on the horizon. Limping slowly into town, we spotted a white stucco cottage camp (a progenitor of today's motels) and thought maybe we could stay there if we had to. Midway along the town's only real street, two or three hundred yards from the "motel," was Glendo's single cafe, where we pulled up to ask about getting help, and something to eat.

The lone waitress appeared tired, depressed, and just a little hostile. When we told her we needed a mechanic, she almost smiled and replied that yes, there was one, even a pair of them, in town, but they had been drunk for the better part of two weeks and were completely out of commission, almost certainly unable to help us. But we pressed her for more information and found out where one of the mechanics lived.

As we headed toward the mechanic's trailer house, we couldn't help but notice how down and depressed everything and everyone seemed to be. All the cowboys and ranchers, wives and children, truckers—everybody—appeared sullen and worried.

A short way from the cafe, we found the drunk mechanic's shabby trailer. I pounded on his door, got no response, but kept on pounding, knowing that he was probably too hungover to wake easily. Eventually, a destroyed-looking guy made it to the door, opening it with eyes blurred and full of hatred for whoever it was that had disturbed him. He looked sick and did his best to get rid of the fresh young honeymooners on his doorstep. But we wouldn't go away and forced him to listen to our tale of woe.

In the end, he weakened and agreed to see what he could do for us—if he could get his partner sober enough to help him. He'd start on our car in the morning if we could drive it a quarter mile to his garage, which was no more than a little falling-down barn with a dirt floor and doors half off their hinges. It didn't look promising, but there was no alternative.

We walked back to the cafe, to our surprise got the car going again, and drove it back to that little motelish sort of place, where we got a tiny room, unloaded our luggage, and collapsed into a much needed though worried nap. In the early evening, we went back to the cafe for a meal. There weren't many customers; those who were there looked dour and depressed. The same waitress who had served us lunch began to take a little interest in us strangers. In a small town like Glendo, strangers are always a matter of interest, if not concern. Glendo didn't get many honeymooners.

The waitress told us what was wrong. There had been a devastating drought—no winter snow and no spring rain. The range had dried up and could no longer support the ranchers' cattle. All the available hay from the preceding year had been fed to the critters in efforts to supplement the desiccated range grasses, so the only thing left to do was drive the cattle to the Glendo railhead, sell them off at a terrible financial loss, and who knows what next? It would be a disaster for Glendo and the area ranches. That's why everyone was so down-in-the-mouth, so dispirited and glum.

A pall hung in the air and was contagious. We began to feel something of the town's despair on top of our own troubles. Funny how in those few hours we had begun to feel a bit like we belonged there.

The next morning, after a fitful and anxious night's sleep in the dreary little room, we found the Chevy willing to start yet one more time, though sounding even worse now that the engine was cold. We got it the short way to the garage, where, lo and behold, both mechanics were waiting, looking as bad as that engine sounded. But they went to work, crawled under the car without benefit of pit or lift, only jacks, and began to remove the pan, where they found the burned-out bearings that had allowed the offending rod to come lose.

In all the doom and gloom, the suffering mechanics under the car would each in turn utter a plaintive "Oh dear!" only to hear a reply of "Oh dear!" in return. I don't know if they fell into that mild and incongruous expletive because there was a lady present, but under the circumstances, we had to smile.

Trouble was, they didn't have the necessary spare parts, would have to get them sent up from Cheyenne by bus, would have to take the extraordinary measure of a long-distance phone call to order them. In those days, long-distance service was unreliable. But they were able to complete the call from the cafe and expected the parts on the Greyhound bus first thing next morning.

We allowed ourselves to be encouraged. Maybe we'd be fixed up and on our way the day after tomorrow.

But "tomorrow" turned out to be another day of waiting, hanging around the cafe, listening to the people who came in, lamenting the drought and what they were going to have to do as a result of it: sell out.

Back at the garage, the mechanics had gotten the engine ready for the new parts, shut down the place, and taken to their beds once again. The evening was long, there was nothing to do, the cafe was closed and the main street dark. People disappeared, back to their dried-up ranches and farms. We felt deserted, and a not little desolate.

We'd barely fallen asleep when we were awakened by what could only be the sound of rain—steady, pouring, drenching, blessed rain. The smell of it came in the window like a balm to our spirits, and we wondered if it would be enough to make a difference to Glendo.

It rained all night, all morning, all day, in fact. That good kind of rain that comes down hard, but still the earth absorbs it, drinking it down deep, where it's needed.

We no more than got to the cafe for breakfast than we could tell that change was in the air. We heard the sounds of hope and expectation now in the conversation of the locals who'd come in. There were even smiles. People began to talk freely to us, as though we'd been in town a long time. It was exciting. If this rain kept up, all might be well. And the rain did keep up, kept on and on, and Glendo was transformed. More and more people showed up at the cafe in celebration. And there we honeymooners were, right in the center of it, sharing the jubilation with this town that had taken us in in our trouble.

I remember feeling privileged to be there with the folks of Glendo, going through this together. Privileged to have our mechanics, who had got the parts off the bus and were even themselves feeling a little better as they worked to re-build our engine. They became almost friendly. What had begun for us as a disaster became our witness to a town's salvation after troubles that made ours seem inconsequential. It was all courtesy of that wonderful, bountiful rain, that water without which the West must fail and die, the water that is the very life of the trout we were going in pursuit of in the old Chevy, our most essential piece of tackle.

The Glendo range would now green up and sustain most of those cattle, allowing them to fatten on the renewed prairie grasses. The ranches, and the families who lived on them, would be saved.

Next morning, after a last breakfast at the cafe, we picked up our repaired and quietly running Chevy, paid our modest bill from our equally modest honeymoon funds, and set out north as the rain kept coming down. We both understood, as we drove out of town past the cafe where we'd begun to feel at home and the garage where we'd been rescued, that our honeymoon, even our marriage, was off to an auspicious beginning. We had gotten our tackle fixed and were ready now to fish in earnest.

And it rained and rained and rained some more all around Glendo.

The Discipline of the Cup

or
How Fishing Improves Character

Betty and I were married in Boulder in June 1948. After the ceremony, we took off north to fish Wyoming's Shoshone River, the rivers of Yellowstone National Park, and the Madison River in Montana. After three weeks of such honeymoon excess, we raced home for the university's summer session, and new-married life.

Only a week later, three old buddies joined Betty and me in laying plans to fish the Woodland Lakes on the edge of the Continental Divide above the Woodland Flats, above Hessie, above Eldora, above Nederland, above Boulder. We hoped that the ice would be out and we'd have little or no trouble with late-remaining snow. With Don, Frank, and Bill, we were five in Bill's Jeep. Scarcely a month earlier, these splendid fellows had stood up with me at my wedding while indulging, I'm sure, their own nuptial fantasies.

Once above Hessie, the outlook for the day began to dim. There was more and more snow. Twice we had to winch ourselves up a bad pitch in the trail, until there was too much snow even for Bill's dauntless Jeep. And so we hiked on in— my three buddies, my bride, and I. Tough going, slogging through the snowfields. We were deeply discouraged to find the upper lake still frozen tight and so made our miserable way down to the lower, smaller lake, which did have a patch of open water that gave up an even more miserable pair of skinny, ten-inch rainbows.

It was past noon and the misery was palpable. On the only bare patch of ground along the lake, on a steep slope, we tried to make camp for lunch. Everything was either sodden or frozen. We could find only a few twigs dry enough to build a fire to make our coffee. The little six-cup pot caught the dour mood of the day and took forever to boil and brew. But finally we got some coffee to go with our sandwiches and so sat on the steep slope of the shore, eating and drinking in glum silence.

Desperate for the coffee, I bolted mine and, half mad with craving, wanted more. With my waders and their suspenders dragging the ground, I moved down to the little fire and the pot with its remaining few drops of the precious stuff. My suspenders caught on one of the longer sticks in the fire, the pot overturned, and the last bit of coffee spilled out, killing the fire into the bargain.

Well, I lost completely whatever temper I had remaining. It was all the tantrum and more that I had the energy to let loose. Betty, my dearest angling bride, sitting just a little up-hill from me, thinking to appease my rage, reached out, offering me her cup with its last few swallows. What gesture could have been sweeter, more generous, more loving?

But not to me. Cursing and carrying on, I grabbed the cup from her and threw its contents out into the lake, and in even greater rage threw myself to the ground to rave on. Then, calm as anything, Betty picked up the empty enameled iron cup that had been mine, and at full arm's length, swung it at me, catching me square on my right temple. I had all I could do, for what seemed like forever, to keep from losing consciousness.

The first thing I saw when I finally regained my wits was my clutch of dear old friends sitting there in stunned horror at the spectacle that had been wrought before them. Could this be a model of the marriage for which they yearned? Was this what it would be like? Poor guys, they were paralyzed with fear and foreboding. Then I looked round to where Betty had been sitting, whence the terrible blow had come. There she was, glowering and silent, utterly unforgiving, arm cocked with the cup, ready to swing again, should I require it.

I want to tell you that my behavior became exemplary on the instant. I became so calm, so agreeable, so congenial, thoughtful, and helpful—in short, I became a model husband right then and there. And I attribute the careful discipline that has marked my behavior during the subsequent fifty-some years of our marriage to that blow of the cup on that miserable day fishing high in the Colorado Rockies.

Don, Bill, and Frank, in that order, went ahead and got married anyway, despite what they had witnessed—such are the hormonal pressures on the young—but I'm sure that my example has stood them in good stead in the years of their enduring marriages.

I don't remember much about the rest of that awful day and the wretched trip home. All I know is that I was exhausted, dismayed, and chastened. Ah yes, chastened. But my character notably improved.

And Betty? Well, to this day she feels that her action on that unhappy fishing trip was altogether appropriate, to say nothing of timely. She, in fact, gave one of those iron cups to each of her daughters as a wedding gift, just in case.

Strawberries on the Coln

A Confession

Sooner or later we confess; we can't keep these things to ourselves forever. If "murder will out," how much more surely will the illicit killing of a fine trout reach confession. On the blissfully happy fishing trip that I'm about to narrate, I did a perfectly awful thing. It was years and years ago, and I remain glad to this day that I did it.

As a young American angler abroad—a thirty-year-old researcher—I dreamed of fishing the fabled chalk streams of Hampshire in southern England. A distinguished member of the staff of the *Sunday Times,* in the garret of whose home we lived in London's Kew Gardens, tried to arrange for me to get on the Test or the Itchen, but to no avail (the English fly-fishing establishment had not in those days discovered the economic advantages of catering to American anglers). Chagrined at his failure, he suggested I try the River Coln in Gloucestershire some eighty miles west of London in the Cotswold hills. After all, the Coln had been the first river mentioned by name in the literature for its trout fishing, and Winston Churchill had fished it. I, too, could get a day ticket from the local hotel and fish its waters.

That first week of July 1958 was right for the river, and besides, I had to clear out of the house in London for a few days to escape the most virulent days of my daughter's mumps. Betty, whose lot it was to remain behind and nurse her, urged me to go, and quickly, but not wearing my Levis.

We were both well aware of the reputation American anglers had attracted in England in those days. The prejudice ran deep against us and our "silly little fly rods" and undignified baseball caps. We agreed that I should undertake the Coln properly dressed—in a three-piece suit of light blue herringbone tweed—an old suit, but correct enough, nicely suppressed at the waist, and with a proper shirt and tie. I felt prepared. With my eight-foot, five-strip Lou Feierabend cane rod, my Colorado/Wyoming flies, and assorted gear, I caught the morning bus from Victoria Station to Fairford in Gloucestershire.

Fairford is a lovely little Cotswold town—a model for country living, in my mind—distinguished by the river and the town's Perpendicular-style Gothic parish church of St. Mary's, as well as the ancient Bull Hotel, which controls fishing rights on the river. The Coln flows at the edge of town, down from Bibury and the famed Arlington Row of "wool houses" a few miles upstream—all of it fine trout water.

The church is marvelous. It dates from the fifteenth century and has the most complete set of narrative painted glass in all of England. The story goes that in the seventeenth century, when the good folk of Fairford got word that Oliver Cromwell was marching westward to do good deeds for Christ, such as destroying all "graven images' of Him, His mother, and His company of saints and martyrs, the Fairfordians removed all the glass piece by piece from their beloved church, took it a couple miles north of town and buried it. Cromwell passed through, disappointed, no doubt, to find no wealth of popish images to destroy, and left after only minimal, random violation of the community. There remained only for the villagers to dig up the colorful glass and replace it in the church window tracery, where it beams and glows and tells its sacred stories to this day.

But to the fishing. I arrived at Fairford in the forenoon and put up at the Bull Hotel. For ten shillings (at the time, just under $2) a day, I got my tickets to fish the river—really a modest-sized chalk stream of perhaps twenty-five feet in average breadth and no great depth. At the hotel desk, I got my instructions, the regulations for fishing the Coln:

1) There will be no wading.
2) Only dry flies, size 12 and smaller may be used.
3) All casts will be made upstream.
4) Casts may not be random, but only to particular, rising fish.
5) No trout under twelve inches may be killed.

Formidable, these rules, but not far from my expectations (I had done my homework). I was anxious to fit into the scene in my herringbone suit, tweed hat, and neutral Colorado English.

I can remember only a blur of activity—checking into the hotel, getting some lunch, and finally pacing through the little town with my tackle to where the stream flows under the main road, at what must have been the ancient "fair ford" itself.

As the water controlled by the hotel lay below the bridge, I started down in that direction, in spite of the fact that I knew my casts must not be downstream. The day was bright, temperate, with only the softest breeze, a perfect late-spring day in the English countryside. For the first time, I heard the beguiling song of the cuckoo. And it didn't take long to spot rising trout.

I tied on a dry fly that I'd developed in Colorado for skittish browns in subalpine lakes—a fly of only a narrow, stiff collar of hackle of variant length, over a full, stiff, extra-long tail. I imagined that the silhouette was especially lifelike, and to be sure, it did float beautifully with its mixed hackles, as select as I could get them. These Coln trout came rather easily and often to this fly, though they insisted on staying just a hair under the legal limit—twelve inches—for keeping.

That first afternoon passed quickly enough once I got properly caught up in the charm, the perfection of it all. The fish I caught became part of the lyric of the stream and its setting—a losing of oneself in the dynamic extension of the fly rod, the curve of the line, and the dance of the fly on the lovely water; a communion with the Cotswolds and the cuckoos gently calling over the meadows.

Having taken perhaps a dozen trout that afternoon and laid plans for the next day to drop down farther on the hotel's water before starting to fish, I went back to the Bull to a pint of the local bitter, a good meal, and a hotel room snug within its sixteenth-century walls.

Saturday morning was as grand as the day before it, and I was eager to be at those browns. By midmorning I was on that lower stretch, new water, when fish began moving to a mayfly that I couldn't at that time identify. But once again my size 16 "impressionist" hackle fly did execution. Move out around, down, and fish up; out around, down, and fish up: that was the pattern.

Suddenly, there it was, looming into my consciousness—the lovely country house right there on the river, down and opposite from me. Like other Cotswold cottages of the local yellowish sandstone, it would date from the sixteenth century, when Henry VIII decided he needed a thriving wool-processing industry to compete with the Flemish. This superb, ancient house, its courses of stone accented with lichens, turned out to be proud enough to have a name of its own—Colnside—and possess, from antiquity, the water and fishing rights within its shadows. The house's long axis lay along the river, its walls set back from the bank by a two-foot-wide stone walkway roughly three feet above the flowing water.

I was thinking that it was my ideal of what a home on a trout stream could be, when a half-door opened from the kitchen and through it stepped a tall, graceful, gray-haired lady in a housedress, carrying a fly rod!

Mrs. Hickman casting from her kitchen door.

I stood rooted to the spot, perhaps two hundred feet up-stream and opposite her as she began to cast her flies over rising fish. What a sight it was, but I'm sorry to report that she was unsuccessful with the fish. Pulling myself together and out of my enchantment, I moved toward her, screwing up my resolve to ask if I might photograph her, her home, and her river. She said that I might.

And one thing led to another. We had a pleasant, brief talk, introduced ourselves, and I took my pictures before she went back into the house. I, in turn, went back to my fishing and my admiration of the details of that wonderful house.

A few minutes later, Mrs. Hickman and her husband emerged at the upstream end of the house to tend their strawberry bed, which I had failed to notice, probably because it lay under netting to keep birds from the ripening berries. From across the river, Mrs. Hickman introduced her husband, somewhat less hardy than she. All the while I was taking trout—all of them that irritating quarter inch under the legal limit. Not that I wanted to kill a bunch of trout for myself, but twelve-plus inches would have given the whole event greater status.

Then it struck me: in spite of the regulations, Mr. and Mrs. Hickman might enjoy the fish I was catching—wasn't she, after all, trying to catch some for herself? Yes, the Hickmans were eager and glad to be offered the fish. And so began one of the most extraordinary spectacles—an idyll, a kind of dance, a transcendent moment in my angler's experience—as I pitched four or more trout across the stream onto the lawn to that elderly couple (remember, wading was prohibited). And they, in turn, tossed back to me gigantic, beautiful strawberries. I think strawberries were never so good. We laughed happily at ourselves and our crazy exchange.

By this time, what with the water, the sun, the trout, catching the brilliant red berries out of the blue of the sky, we had begun to inquire into each other's lives. They got from me that I was a Fulbright scholar in London with a wife and mump-swollen daughter left behind, an American from the Wild West intent on English trout and the secret of why English Shakespearean acting was what it was.

Nothing would do, said Mrs. Hickman, but that I should come the next day for Sunday dinner. Having given instructions on how to come down the other side of the Coln next day, they covered their strawberry bed and went in. I went back to my fishing, only slightly guilt-ridden about my river piracy on behalf of the Hickmans.

Then happened the principal matter of this confession. Fifty yards upstream from Colnside loomed an ancient willow whose branches reached down into the river, forming a dark cavern that faced upstream, with a two-foot window into it. Everything inside me said that I had to put a really meaty fly into that darkness. A big brown had to be down in there, waiting and on the prod.

In a spate of nerves, I tied on a size 6 Muddler Minnow, stepped into the water to the tops of my high shoes to get a good casting vantage above the hole, and, steeling myself for the single cast I knew I'd be allowed, I slammed the Muddler like a grasshopper down the fifty feet and, to my profound surprise and satisfaction, right through that opening into the darkness.

Simply all hell broke loose.

As my guilty good fortune would have it, the trout came tearing straight out of the tangle and into open water, where he fought the good fight before folding into the landing net—all of his fifteen inches and nearly two pounds. A trout-of-crime. I'd broken every rule, defied all the regulations. I'd cast downstream and to the water, not to a rising fish. I'd used a big fly. A wettish fly of a streamer sort to boot. I was even standing in the river. The only legal aspect of the event was the size of the trout: here at last was a fish for the bag.

As my luck would continue to have it, the river keeper was nowhere to be seen. We'd met earlier in the day and had exchanged courtesies. I was glad now that he wasn't around to haul me in for "courtesies" of another sort.

In the meantime, Mrs. Hickman had come out again, noted my fine fish and sang its praises, never suggesting that she knew the depth of my infamy in taking it. She promised to pack it for me to carry back to London when I came for dinner the next day.

The fish was nicely heavy in my bag for the rest of the afternoon, until a storm came up to find me taking refuge under a tree with a London angler who had entered the river from below. He tried to be encouraging by allowing that the trout should rise again at tea time. But they didn't. The fishing appeared to be over. My companion of the storm and I made our way back upriver to the hotel and the cozy public house next door, where the whiskey was particularly good. I remember that when we both had had enough—not of fishing or each other but of whiskey—we went out to his car, only to discover a flat tire. We were silly drunk enough to make fools of ourselves trying to discover the operative principle of his jack—all in vain—until a local lad came by and rescued us from our shame.

After considerable and undignified carryings-on, my new London angling friend set off for home and I for the hotel desk to check in for the measurement and recording of my fish. This trout subsequently proved to be the best of that season—a nice boast for me but not for the river, I thought. Churchill had caught bigger ones back then—a photo at the desk was proof.

Oh, I bluffed it out all right. I think I said that I'd taken the fish on a number 18 "BWO" or something like that. Anyhow, the crime had been committed, and I was willing to accept whatever glory it might afford.

And so to bed, after another good dinner and the prospect of tomorrow's meal with the Hickmans at noon, followed by the bus ride back to London.

Sunday dawned fine but somehow different—a day to do other things until time to head home. So, after what was in those remote days still a full English breakfast with kippers and all, I wandered around Fairford for photographs—especially of the wonderful church of St. Mary's. I heard the music of the morning service and walked out of town to see the obelisk marking the spot where the citizens had buried their stained glass those centuries earlier.

Back to the hotel to pick up my trout and go to Hickman's for dinner. A fifteen-minute walk took me to Colnside, where the joint was a roast of pork, a solid English Sunday dinner at its best. A door from the dining room opened out onto the river, and as we ate, the trout steadily worked the water, sipping away at some tiny mayfly or other. After a dessert of trifle and coffee, Mrs. Hickman produced a large candy box full of extra-select strawberries exquisitely packed in their own leaves for my wife and daughter back in London. She then packed my fifteen-inch brown in another box of strawberry leaves. No trout was ever more prettily bedded—not on land at least.

It was wonderful. I gave Mrs. Hickman some three dozen of my flies—even four Muddlers, on the possibility, I suppose, that if she should come to use these big flies, some of my guilt would be assuaged, my sin absolved. She was enthusiastic about them. We promised to exchange Christmas cards as I left to catch my bus.

The ride back was uneventful until we reached the outskirts of London, where the driver learned that I was not to be picked up at the suburban station close to Kew Gardens. Nothing would do but that he should push his bus through the tiny streets and tight turns almost to my door at Westhall, our house in Kew. I was flushed with gratitude.

So, now I've confessed to both my crime and my extraordinary pleasure in those few days, that one fish, and those good people the Hickmans, who had no prejudice at all, it seemed, about American anglers. They are gone now.

Not too long ago I had occasion to pass through Fairford again, long enough to look around, even to fish for a morning. The water, the trout, the church, the hotel are all still much as they were then and had remained in my memory since 1958. The house itself, Colnside, I'm sorry to say, has suffered unfortunate additions and now appears to be just another West-of-England house.

Finally, with a bit of perverse pride, I add that there is to this day at the hotel desk that record book, which will attest that the best fish of the 1958 season was mine, no one the wiser that it was a thoroughly illicit achievement by that American in the blue herringbone suit.

Two Donegal Salmon

We were going to Ireland at last. For almost a year in London, we had dreamed of such a pilgrimage, of getting to the Abbey Theatre in Dublin, tangling with at least one Atlantic salmon, and generally catching the spirit and beauty of the place. But first, the three of us—me, my wife Betty, and our six-year-old daughter Linnea, had to cross the Irish Sea on the rolling, pitching tub of a mail boat from Holyhead in Wales to Dublin's docking at Dun Laoghaire. I was sick as a horse all night long on the heavy seas, the ladies having pilled themselves in order not to be.

Coming ashore wan and weary, we were shocked to find Ireland under a full foot of new snow. Dublin itself, that March morning, was all but shut down and unearthly quiet. We picked up our rented car, got lost and confused in the snow and obscure streets, stopped long enough by the Grand Canal for Linnea and me to snowball the white gulls on the black water, and eventually located our B&B. Once we'd settled in, it was back out into the snow to see what sights we could.

In the center of town we located places like the General Post Office, Stephen's Green, and Trinity College, sacred to the pilgrim in Ireland. Next day, the Abbey Theatre, which we learned was in decline and living in rented Queen's Theatre, proved disappointing.

Then we got to worrying about how the snow would affect the fishing on the Bundrose River to the northwest, in county Donegal. Our reservations at the Hamilton Hotel promised great March runs of fresh salmon. But to be on the safe side, we wired the hotel and heard back that we could and maybe should delay our arrival by several days.

And so we filled three days driving south out of the snow and into the lovely countryside clear down to Cork before heading up north through spectacular Connemara, along the rugged and superb west coast, through County Mayo and the Yeats country, and on into wild and remote Donegal. All was brilliant green, blue, and russet, just the way Ireland ought to look with St. Patrick's Day nearly upon us.

Our hotel, on the main road through the little town of Bundoran, stood just across the street from the Atlantic and its hard-breaking seas. Mr. Hamilton himself welcomed us warmly, but with disappointing reports of the fishing. Few salmon were being killed. He blamed the icy wind blowing, he said, out of Russia.

Entering the hotel, we noticed right away the fine ten-pounder, fresh as anything, that lay on an elegant silver tray in the reception hallway. We were instructed that such was the practice, to display every afternoon each guest's catch of the day in anticipation of its likely preparation for one of the hotel's excellent dinners. It should be noted that one half of everyone's catch was the hotel's property, used by the chef to feed us or sell at market.

Several of Mr. Hamilton's regular guests were there for the fishing and proved marginally cordial to a barely thirtysomething American interloper and his family, who, after all, only wanted a few of their beloved salmon. Betty, an experienced angler herself, was giving up the chance (and the expense) to fish in favor of caring for our daughter and urging me on.

Mr. Hamilton scheduled me to fish the upper beat of the river the following day. A day's fishing cost the angler one pound sterling, and with my ghillie at another pound, plus his lunch and a bottle of Guinness, as well as a state license, expenses mounted—though good salmon fishing still cost less here than anywhere else.

I had thought it best in London to rent a proper salmon fly rod, reel, and line at a shop in St. James's Street. It was a fourteen-foot beast that felt almost too heavy to carry, let alone cast. But I had a backup—my own powerful eight-and-a-half-foot, five-strip stick, not to mention a sturdy spinning rig. Either way, I was certain that I was well equipped to whip any salmon alive.

My young ghillie, an agreeable sort, insisted on carrying the big salmon rod from place to place and provided the flies, the first one a beat-up Thunder and Lightning. He bent it to the heavy leader and told me just where to toss it—instruction the likes of which I've never quite learned to enjoy.

All day long and not a smell. Nothing but a single ugly kelt about a yard long and no bigger around than my skinny wrist. The ghillie was reluctant even to touch this horribly spent salmon that had survived spawning and had now to feed hard or die. Folklore about kelts holds that they are poisonous to eat. That was it on this bitterly cold, wind-driven day.

Waiting back at the car, Betty and Linnea had spent the day walking, reading, and generally killing time. They had been sitting on the riverbank when a gypsy mother and child approached and dunned them for loose change. These true Irish gypsies, rather threatening, if not dangerous, with their menfolk in sight at their caravan, disconcerted Betty, who had no idea how to deal with them. When at last she made it clear that she carried no money, the woman and child sullenly went away. It had been quite uncomfortable.

Back at the hotel, after a warm-up and a bit of a rest, we enjoyed a fine dinner, accompanied as it was by a colorful lecture from a fellow guest, the equally colorful Commander, at the next table, on the virtue of the long fly rod over what he deemed our pitifully inadequate short American rods. The

Commander, exactly the stereotypical British military gentleman one might imagine him to be, was a regular at the hotel, presided both at dinner and on the Bundrose. He knew all the river's beats intimately and was persuasive in his contention that it didn't make as much difference how far one could cast a salmon fly as it did what the angler could do with the fly in the water. With the long rod one could swim the fly deftly through every pocket, rip, and riffle, all under precise control. The short rod didn't allow that. Perhaps the current American interest in spey rods bears out the Commander's gruff assessment. He also insinuated his stern disapproval of my having my family along on such a trip. His wife, he gave me to understand, was properly in France, collecting Gothic churches.

Daughter Linnea, a real trooper, was fast getting sick, something like flu. It was a worry, but next morning we felt we could both care for her and keep going ourselves. So, on the advice of Mr. Hamilton, who declared it senseless to fish that windy, cold morning, we drove farther north into the wilder parts of coastal Donegal—in fact, across the border into Ulster, soon to trouble all Irish people so terribly.

I was beginning to get discouraged, even depressed, about the fishing and didn't much look forward to returning to the hotel for an afternoon's fishing, even at half price: ten shillings for half a day. The morning's sightseeing drive had been so beautiful and interesting in the warm car that beating the water for a fish in the raw cold didn't much appeal. And when, that afternoon, I did get back on the river, I didn't see a sign of a fish.

Betty sensed that I was ready to give up, throw in the towel, and got extremely businesslike with me. She told me I had to keep after it, keep fishing. She urged me to insist that next day Hamilton put me on the lowest beat on the river, right where it dumps into the Atlantic, where the only recent fish had been taken. Dinner conversation around the dining room tables bore out that that beat alone was worth fishing.

We were beginning to suspect Mr. Hamilton had been saving that good water for his regulars instead of wasting it on us drop-in Americans, whom he would likely never see again.

So, I confronted our host and pressed him to give me a crack at the bottom beat. He agreed, most likely feeling a little guilty about us by then. Tomorrow—St. Patrick's Day, in fact—he would take me down there, within walking distance of the hotel, himself. He was none too cheerful about it, sure as he was that in this Russian weather we would do no good.

In despair of flies ever working for me, I told him I wanted to throw some hardware, and use my own spinning tackle that a year before had killed a big Rogue River Chinook. Spinning was fine with him, but he urged that I use what is perhaps the most famous of all British hardware, the Devon Minnow, a torpedo shape of metal with minnow finish and propeller blades at the head, spinning on a wire shaft. He would be happy to sell me a couple.

Betty was satisfied that I had not given up, and I even began to feel a bit hopeful, what with the possibility of a blessing from the great Irish saint the next day. And so we took to our comfortable but none-too-warm room for the night. Tomorrow, après fishing, we would have to return to Dublin.

That last day of our stay dawned bright, cold, and breezy, and after one of those magnificent Irish breakfasts the likes of which I yearn for nearly every day of my life, we were on the river at nine, chucking a Devon Minnow slightly upstream, swinging it down so close to the Atlantic breakers that I could have reached them easily with a long downriver cast. It was a wild and beautiful prospect, an idealization of the west coast of Ireland. The river was maybe fifty feet wide, deep, without much structure, and moving right along, slightly tea-colored. I got the hang of the Devon quickly and, to Mr. Hamilton's stunned surprise, was into a fish right away. The bright, fresh salmon came to Mr. Hamilton's net without trouble and to his great satisfaction—I might even say delight—because it enabled him now to suggest that we pack it in and return to the warmth of the hotel. I, on the other hand, desperately wanted another fish, because, it must be remembered, half of that one fish I'd just killed belonged to Mr. Hamilton. We could halve it and each keep a half, or I could pay him Dublin market price for his and take the entire fish for my own. Whichever I wanted. But on our meager finances, we couldn't afford that. Besides, I wanted a whole fish to take back to London—without paying more for it than I had already.

Well, again I insisted and refused to give up. I flung that Devon upriver once again, and, would you believe it, on that very next cast, another fish took, and almost at once ran under a snag of brush in the river. That did it. Mr. Hamilton was sure the fish was impossibly tangled and should be broken off so we could get ourselves back to the hotel posthaste.

I again wanted none of his counsel. I told him, "Naw, let's do what we sometimes do with a snagged fish back in the Rockies." He wondered what in the world that might be. When he learned that it was merely to throw the fish lots of slack line, sit down on the bank, and wait for the fish to untangle itself, he thought I must be crazy.

But we did it anyway. I stretched out full length, trying to gather a little warmth from the wan sun and to concentrate on the extraordinary circumstances that sometimes take command of our lives, while the fish worked at freeing itself from the mess it was in. Come free it did and, after powering around a bit, gave up to the net. Mr. Hamilton was all amazement and gratification, because now we could surely go in, which we did. I had twin twelve-pound, fresh-from-the-salt, dazzlingly blue-silvered salmon: one for him and one for me— for Betty, Linnea, and me, that is. Maybe St. Patrick hadn't personally arranged my good luck, but he couldn't have hurt.

Betty was as pleased as could be. Linnea was feeling better and walked across the road from the hotel with me so Betty could photograph us with the fish, the Atlantic, looking out toward America, our backdrop.

I'd brought with me from London, as an act of faith, one of those woven-grass salmon-sized carrying bags with a simple web handle—just the thing for our return home. The first leg of the journey was a short afternoon's drive across the center of Ireland, back to Dublin, which we were shocked again to find all but shut down and unearthly quiet until we learned that it was always that way on St. Patrick's Day afternoon, after the morning's parade. But it was a beautiful, dreamlike sort of quiet. We drove around at ease, taking photographs of a city deeply at rest.

Then it was a rush to catch the late afternoon sailing of the mail boat back to Holyhead, and to be sick all over again. But not sick enough to allow the salmon out of our sight.

Mr. Hamilton had confided in me before we left the hotel that, though he regretted to say it, a salmon was fair game for thieves anywhere, and we should guard ours diligently.

That we did. That fish was worth more than ten pounds on the market—a lot of money back then, at least for us.

Ashore at Holyhead we boarded the London-bound night train, which just sat there and sat there until midnight while we froze nearly do death, until it was explained that the train's "driver" had for some arcane labor reason refused to show up to "drive" the train to London. At last a substitute was found, but we were hours late and exhausted when we pulled into Euston Station. The salmon had been in the luggage rack right over my head all the way; now it faced the Underground ride across London to our flat in Kew Gardens.

It had been a great trip. We had met Ireland head on and loved it. I had laid the foundations of a lifelong professional specialty in Irish theatre and drama. Linnea was well again and back in school. Betty had made me stick with the fishing and get what I so dearly wanted: those two Donegal salmon—one for the hotel to feed to its guests and one for Betty to feed to the three of us. I should have liked them both to have come to a fly instead of to hardware, but "travelers must be content."

A Tale of Trout Lake

It was late April 1953. My friend Herb Wolsborn, mathematician for Northwest Community College in Powell, Wyoming, by profession and photographer by avocation, got a call from a Yellowstone Park wildlife biologist he knew saying, "Come on up to the Lamar River meadows near Soda Butte, and come fast. The elk are calving all over the place, and the calves have to be tagged right after the cows drop 'em. We want you to photograph the operation for us." Herb asked if he might bring a friend—meaning me—and was told that he could. And so we took off from Powell, where I was teaching at the high school, on Friday afternoon for a long weekend up in the northeast corner of Yellowstone. I, who wouldn't be caught anywhere in that neck of the woods without my fishing tackle, stashed it on board Herb's van, just in case.

In those days it was a tough trip to Cook City, and on that Friday the red mud at the base of Dead Indian Hill was almost impassable. Farther up still, the road was icy, but make it we did.

That Saturday on the Lamar meadows there were a lot of elk cows and calves—rather too much the same thing over and over for me, but for Herb the challenge of getting good pictures kept him happily on assignment. In some frustration, I asked one of the biologists if he knew of any good fishing nearby and was told that there was a little pond nearby, hidden away, that almost no one fished—Trout Lake, half a mile up a steep pitch off the main highway along the Lamar.

Sounded good to me. And so, next morning, leaving Herb to his Leica and the elk, I slogged through the late-remaining snow and mud up to Trout Lake, found it easily enough but awful to fish, with its steep banks. But good grief, the lunker trout that were constantly cruising by! Rainbows, lazing deep off that bowl-like, precipitous shoreline. Scads of them.

The round little two-acre lake lay in a pristine meadow in a saddle of the mountains, offering no sign that anyone had been there before me—unless you could count a cow and calf moose between whom I stupidly managed to insert myself. I knew I'd made a terrible mistake and was probably going to be trampled to death by the old lady. Mercifully, though—and I'll never know why—she let me walk out of my entrapped position before turning away with her young one and lumbering in that ungainly moosian way back into the timber. Such was my luck that day.

That luck allowed me to get off a few good casts and nail four of those sixteen- to twenty-inch rainbows. But it was clear that I just wasn't able to get my fly down deep enough, fast enough, or keep it there long enough to do the work as I knew it must be done. But what a discovery this pond was. I was nearly out of my head.

Back at ranger headquarters later in the day, I spilled it all to Herb, who was suitably impressed. Right then and there we planned to return with some sort of boat that would get us out and away from those steep banks. Next time, we'd bring lines that would sink. Notice that I did not say "sinking lines," because there were no such things in those primitive times. But there were those so-called "floating" nylon fly lines that would sink no matter how they were cleaned and dressed, and those we had. I, however, had something even better, my secret weapon.

Two weeks later, in an awful hurry, Herb and I put the trip to Trout Lake together, borrowed a pitiful old World-

War-II-surplus, three-man rubber life raft that had been patched and repatched again but was safe enough, we felt, for this small lake. An ancient Coleman stove, an overgrown pup tent, sleeping bags, enough to eat, dry socks, lots of tackle, and our high hearts: such was the gear that we packed into Herb's rough and ready Chevy van.

This time, the trip up over Dead Indian Hill was easier, the red mud nearly dry, but still it was a three-hour drive to the northeast entrance of the park. Around Soda Butte, about a mile above where the trail to Trout Lake took off from the highway, was a campground typical of that day in its meager facilities. We took what we thought was a good spot, set up our tent, readying it as fully as we dared, given the marauding Yellowstone bears, for our return at the end of the day, and hurried away to get fishing.

Down the road at the pulloff below the lake, we found it no easy task to lug that clumsy boat, along with everything else, up the steep, slippery trail to Trout Lake. We must have looked pretty sad. But fortunately there was no one to see us, and so we soldiered on under our burden, buoyed by our expectation of some really great fishing.

Coming out of the timber at the southeast corner of the lake, we plumped down on the raft to rest a minute but were immediately drawn to our feet again by the spectacle in the water beneath us: trout after big trout cruising by, more, even, than I'd promised Herb he'd see. In no time we were rigging tackle and hauling the boat to a place where we could launch it.

Now, about that "secret weapon": I had an ancient, worn-out, barren-of-finish, once aristocratic Hardy Corona fly line. This grand old line was van Dyke brown oiled silk, size A— or rather that part of it that I'd spliced as a shooting head onto monofilament shooting line in the manner of the San Francisco lads who were at that time setting the pace for the rest of the world's flycasters with their innovations. This beat-up old line had been given me, for its souvenir value, by an old past-master Colorado fly fisherman who had worn it out years before and surely never imagined that I'd actually fish it.

Anyway, I knew that this line would sink like a rock, and nearly as fast. And what's more, it would enable me to swim my unweighted fly parallel to the bottom, down as deep as fifteen feet, just off the weeds. It was this working the fly parallel to the bottom and avoiding too early a climb to the surface that would be the secret of success. I'd learned that over on Henry's Lake in Idaho and was willing to bet that it would be the ticket here, on Trout Lake.

Once we were out on the water, this tactic proved just right. My size 6 Jungle Hornet, decked out with its spectacular four pairs of jungle cock nails, got me into heavy rainbows at once, almost one after another. They'd stop my retrieve with a shoulder-wrenching strike, or maybe follow the fly, slow and easy, until it began to rise toward the boat, and then, sometimes within the leader's length, nearly tear me to pieces with their strikes.

Nothing under two pounds; nothing over four. For maybe a half hour Herb went through some heavy frustration while waiting for his line to soak up and sink deep enough, but my old Corona soaked up in an instant and must then have weighed in the range of a #12 or #13 modern fly line. The big five-strip rod I was waving handled it pretty well, however.

That extravagant jungle cock, Atlantic-salmon creation of a fly (to this day I can't imagine why I chose to start out with it) was too soon chewed up and broken off, after which we found that a largish fly with a peacock body and brown hackle—a sort of proto–Zug Bug—was irresistible to those fish. We caught 'em till our arms ached. Our arms ached even worse when, every hour or so, we had to make for shore, rowing that ridiculous, half-submerged old raft like a couple of clowns in order to pump it up again before it sank, taking us with it. But each time, we'd get back on the water in a hell of a hurry because the fishing was getting faster and faster as the day wore on. Now we had to figure out how to handle those great trout when we were both on at the same time.

How many we caught I hesitate to say, but we kept three apiece for the table—the sort of thing we could still do with impunity back in those days.

It was hard work whipping those fish and managing that raft that didn't want to hold air. By late afternoon we were beat and thinking of camp and its consolations, meager as they would be.

And so, we dragged the raft up from the lake and organized our gear for the stumble back down the trail to the car, lugging those six big trout in a gunnysack. We noted with trepidation that the heavens were working up for a punishing storm, a real dilly, it looked like. And it was. It caught us halfway down the trail and nearly washed us away. In only moments we were soaked through and seriously cold, the wind driving its chill deep into our marrowbones. Lashing the obstreperous raft to the top of the Chevy van was almost more than we could accomplish in the wind and rain. But do it, somehow, in our despair, we did. Then it was a short drive, in the gathering dark, back to the campground, to the miserable little tent where we would have to spend the night.

Jungle Hornet

The last scene of this story takes place in that tent during that awful night. We secured the van as quickly as possible and piled into the tent, taking most of the rain and cold in with us, or so it seemed. Our only light came from two flashlights and a candle. We hadn't thought we'd have to do anything but sleep within the tight confines of the tent. We couldn't sit up and couldn't move around, as there was no place to move to. In spite of the peril it posed, we fired up the old Coleman and got out of our wet clothes and into whatever dry stuff we'd brought along.

The prospects of a decent dinner within the tent were bleak indeed. I was as miserable as I could remember being. Not even the thought of the wonderful fishing that had filled our day could cheer me. But my despair was not to last. Out of the corner of my downcast eye, I noticed that half-sly, half-silly grin that always came across Herb's face when he was up to something. With that grin he would also raise an index finger as if to say, "Just wait." This he did now as he began rummaging in his duffel, looking for what, I couldn't even begin to imagine. But he was clearly up to something.

In a moment he pulled that something out of the bag, holding it on high and pointing at it, with that characteristic grin all over his face. It was a small, old-fashioned medicine bottle stopped with cork, full of what proved to be bourbon. That great amber spirit of all sour mashes that hath power to infuse its spirit into the spirit of man in his hour of direst need. And our need was dire enough for sure.

In no time we were savoring a couple ounces of it from our iron cups, enough to restore us to our pleasure. Images of our fishing began to return, coming in a rush: the striking, hooking, fighting, and landing of as many particular fish as we could recall. The dark tent seemed light enough now. Herb had saved the day, as he'd saved many a day before with just such a small, restorative gesture. It was his reputation among all those who knew him.

And so, we set about getting our dinner of pork chops, which turned out to be better than, minutes before, we would ever have dreamed possible. The boiled coffee was superb and, followed by yet another sip at the bourbon, made everything exactly right.

Still, lest you think that Herb and I experienced unremitting joy, I have to add that as we got down into our sleeping bags and were about to nod off, the damned bears wandered into camp and came snuffling, huffing, and bumping around our tent, keeping at it all night. God, how we hated those bears! A night's sleep lost in fear and frustration, since there was nothing we could do but wait them out and hope for the best.

But with the dawn, the warm sun, bacon and eggs, and another half day of fishing ahead—which proved a repeat of the day before—we were able to look back on that first day with the particular satisfaction that fishermen and good friends sometimes are allowed to know—when they saw their work and did it. In the end, neither a leaky boat, bad weather, nor any number of bears could spoil that experience now so dearly engraved onto memory.

Fishing Poolside

There I was, of an April Saturday morning years ago, standing at the side of Powell High School's swimming pool, togged out in full angling regalia, about to attach a snap-swivel to an eyelet in the back of a web belt around a two-hundred-pound, six-foot-four, All-American swimmer. I had boasted that I could land him on a 3X leader tippet in one hour.

The whole thing had begun maybe four months earlier as I daily heard the coaches in the faculty lounge talking their trade. The addition of University of Wyoming All-American swimmer Dennis Brittain to the group somehow led me at last to barge in and state my claim that any swimmer could be landed on the proper fly-fishing tackle. Of course, no one believed me. The talk went on through late winter and early spring until the inevitable happened. Another teacher, tired of hearing about it, butted in with,

"Why don't you guys shut up and try it?" Well, the gage was down, and I had to pick it up.

Plans were laid for that Saturday morning in April. I required that Brittain not touch the edges of the pool nor stand on the bottom. And, of course, he must not touch the leader with his hands. Unfortunately for me, he talked me into halving the allotted time to thirty minutes. I agreed, but reluctantly, knowing that my only chance was to go very, very slowly with him. We agreed on a means of attaching the leader to him at his waist.

As Powell, in those days, was a town of fewer than four thousand souls, rumor of our contest got around quickly and thoroughly. *The Powell Tribune* picked up the story and wrote about us. There was considerable interest all over town.

But what we didn't know was that the newspaper had put the story out on the wire, and as a result, one evening I got a call from *Life* magazine. An editor proposed to fly out a writer and a photographer to cover the proceedings. Was that okay with me? Well, sure. How could I refuse? But when they arrived early the Friday before the big event, the picture began to change. Would I agree to dress fully as for the stream, waders and all? Could we have cheerleaders for each side of the contest? At some point, would I jump down into the pool (shallow end) and fight Dennis from there? It was turning into a big production. Still, we agreed, with the exception of my jumping into the pool. I knew that I would need to keep vertical leverage on Dennis and remain free to move around the perimeter of the pool with him. I said only that I *might* jump in.

And so, there we were on that Saturday morning, scheduled to begin the duel at exactly eleven. The pool gallery was full to overflowing with students, townspeople, faculty—all sorts. There was great noise and carrying-on. The cheerleaders were at their work while placard signs, exhorting the crowd to take sides, were paraded around.

Hoping to unnerve my adversary a bit, like a medieval torturer, I showed him the instruments: my powerful

Feierabend five-strip cane rod of eight-and-half feet, the big four-by-one-inch Pflueger salmon-model Medalist reel, and a double-A belly shooting head—a #10 weight by AFTM standards. My leader of nine feet went down to a .008-inch, 3X point, not as strong by half back then as it is today.

I was feeling pretty nervous myself, especially about giving up half an hour to my adversary. With time now on his side, I'd have to be very careful yet very persuasive with that big rod.

So the eleventh hour came round at last. Dennis and I were at the shallow end of the pool, ready to go. The official timers were at their table. At precisely eleven, the head swimming coach raised the starting pistol as master swimmer and accomplished athlete Brittain slipped down into the pool.

At the sound of the pistol, he made three or four lazy, graceful short excursions here and there in the water, in response to which the Medalist reel sang out prettily. He was working his way in an attractive pattern—a handsome sight to behold—to the middle of the pool, where suddenly he went dead in the water. That got me really nervous. Even the gallery fell silent with heightened expectation. All I could do was wonder, point the tip of the rod directly at him, glance at the way the line was spooling on the reel, and hang on.

I never saw what happened. There was only this immense thrashing of the water, like a monster whale sounding with a parting smash on the surface as it disappeared into the depths. My reel cried out in a spasm of anguish and went silent. I felt that spasm in my bowels and, for my pains, got line and leader snapped back into a puddle at my feet. Dennis had been in the water barely a minute.

Talk about feeling disgraced!

The crowd was disgruntled. I'd put up no show at all. Surely the men from *Life,* who had been taking pictures a mile a minute, must have feared that their story was stillborn. As I tried to slink away into the obscurity of my own part of the building—the theatre—now feeling perfectly absurd in waders and all that gear, the *Life* men nabbed Dennis and me

to try some set-ups in the pool that might save our story for publication. In our obliging way, we did as they wanted, shame-faced though I was.

It didn't take long for me to realize where I had miscal-culated. I had not taken into account human intelligence. While Brittain was loafing out there in the center of the pool, he was working out a strategy based on his analysis of my technical weaknesses and his having preyed so nicely on my nerves. No damned fish can do that! If we anglers aren't able to think like a fish, it's certain that no fish can think, analyze, and then act like a human being, like a Dennis Brittain, who simply figured me out and did me in. There were other contributing factors, of course. I ought never to have used a big bellied fly line, with its heavy drag in the water. The leader ought to have been attached low at the back of the swimmer's neck— a connection more like that to a fish. And I ought to have been less dramatic about the whole thing—and less nervous, less hurried.

In the end, *Life* didn't publish the piece. We were disappointed as we watched for it during the weeks of that late spring. And I felt rather bad, as though I'd suckered everybody in town. On the other hand, we all had a good time, and I still think it just might be possible to succeed.

As I look back on it now, more than thirty years later, it seems wonderful that a crazy, spontaneous thing like that could have taken place and been so exciting an occasion in the life of a community. And that's the thing: that little Wyoming town was a genuine community with an extraordinary genius all its own—full of soul as well as souls. There, almost anything was possible.

In an Irish May

Early in May, Irish anglers get a little soft-focused and more than a little restless as they look forward to the rebirth of the Mayfly, *Ephemera danica,* the grandest mayfly of them all. Over there, *Mayfly* is a proper noun only when it refers to that single insect *E. danica,* known as the Green Drake in its dun or *sub-imago* phase—just like its counterpart in the U.S.—and as Spent Gnat when a spinner or *imago.* Why Green Drake? We learn in Charles Cotton's contribution to Walton's *Compleat Angler,* that it's because of the way its setae curve up like a mallard drake's curly tail feathers. So then, just as the unadorned word *fish* means "salmon" to the Irish folk of the west, so a Mayfly is always and only the big, beautiful *E. danica* that hatches late in May and into June, to the deep satisfaction and reward of every angler.

When this hatch is up, as the Irish say, it's something to behold: a spectacle of wonder and beauty to take one's breath away. When the Irish fisher sees the first Mayfly of the season, he says in Irish (or at least he ought to say), *"Go mbeimid beo ag an am seo aris"*—May we live to see this great thing at this same time next year."

One of my Irish months of May found me in County Galway, all set up for four days with the salmon at the famous weir over the River Corrib, just below where it flows from the immense and fabled Lough Corrib and makes its short run to the sea through old and mysterious Galway City.

My host was the noted fisheries administrator and one-time head of intelligence in the Irish army, Colonel Edward Cusack. True to Ned's promise, the salmon ran well, and I caught my share of sea-bright eight- to ten-pounders. To add to the excitement of those salmon days, word was bruited about that the Mayfly was beginning to appear here and there. Ned's plans were for us to go out on Lough Corrib to dap the live Mayfly—that age-old way of angling—in expectation of the heavy, roundish-bodied browns that are the ancient pride of that water.

But first we were to have yet another go at the salmon in a river up in Connemara, the lovely Ballynahinch. On the way, driving north through the town of Oughterard, I puzzled over the boys standing around at crossroads and in front of shops, motionless, expressionless, holding small chests, a little bigger than cigar boxes, with air holes in them. When I wondered aloud what these boys were doing and why they weren't in school, Ned stopped the car so we could get out and approach the shy, silent boys. I was astonished to learn that they were holding live-boxes full of Mayflies—big, beautiful, graceful Green Drakes of that impossible-to-classify, faintly greenish tint. These boys had picked the living flies off the foliage at the lake's edge the evening before and were selling them to fishermen at fifty newpence the dozen. We might have bought flies right then and gone dapping on Corrib that very day, but for this side trip to the famed Ballynahinch.

Full of the pleasure of the moment, I thought these boys with their Mayflies made one of the most beguiling scenes in all my fisherman's experience—something I had never in the world expected, these Irish lads, out of their schoolrooms to peddle the great duns in the streets of their small Irish town.

But we had to hurry on. The salmon were waiting in the Ballynahinch, and the boys would be there tomorrow when we needed their flies for dapping on Lough Corrib.

When we arrived at Ballynahinch Castle, now an exclusive fishing lodge near the rise of the short, coastal river, we met an old fishing partner of the Colonel's, the riverkeeper there. He kept us from the river long enough to tell us in lengthy detail, much of it in exuberant Irish, about how just the week gone by, a giant of a salmon had hit his point fly, gotten soundly hooked, fought, and during the fight, out of pure and righteous anger, turned and took the dropper fly as well. The castle lodge and the pints of Guinness conspired with Michael's "gallous" story to delay a bit our getting on the river, but that was okay with us.

After that it was all downhill—down to the river and down on our luck. We rigged our flies to fifteen-foot graphite rods on a gorgeous stretch of water where Michael said he'd seen fish. I was certain I'd hang one that morning. Everything felt right. But nothing, not a smell. My casts were dead. Ned had gone off downriver, out of sight.

After half an hour, Betty, who had accompanied us on the trip, heard him calling for me to come fast with the net. When I caught up with him, he was going full tilt toward the Atlantic behind a great fish. In maybe thirty minutes, Ned had him stopped down under a very steep, high bank. It was for me to find a way down the gorse-covered ledge to the fish. It wasn't easy. The gorse hurt a lot, and the footing was terrible, but get down I did. And there was that monster cock salmon wallowing in a pocket at the shore. Surely, we thought, he would be at least twenty pounds.

Scared to death by the responsibility, I worked the net under him and tried to calculate exactly the right moment to hoist, quick and sure. And when I did, the damned net broke at the ferrule where the hoop joined the long handle. The exhausted fish got dumped right out of the net and back into a current that broke him off and carried him, drifting on the surface, exhausted, downriver to the sea, around the next bend. It was awfully quiet around there for the rest of that midday, with Ned murmuring soft, reassuring things to cheer me up. And it was *his* fish that *I'd* lost for him. I'll never cease wondering how I might have handled that net differently, and gotten that fish well dispatched high up on the bank, where Ned stood staring blankly toward the ocean. Oh, the grief of it!

But this is a story about the Mayfly.

I'd first encountered the Mayfly on the Kells Blackwater north of Dublin one May several years earlier, again with my friend Ned. I say *Kells* Blackwater because Ireland has two rivers of that name, the northern one rising just west of Kells and flowing east. It's hard to describe what took place that morning when I got rigged up and on the river. The duns were coming down nicely, an enchanting sight. Standing in about ten inches of water, I noticed the drakes around my wadered legs and knelt in the water to try to see them emerge. But, for the life of me, I couldn't. I put my face to the water, held my breath, and stared at the surface, determined to see one of the long, thin nymphs swim to the surface, break from its shuck, and emerge whole and perfect. But no luck. Time and again, this gorgeous insect suddenly appeared, rested for an instant, and then sailed off with the wind. Why could I not see the moment of birth, or rather, transformation? The experience was close to miraculous.

In fact, everything about the Mayfly in Ireland is surrounded with mystery and mythic resonance, beyond entomology and strict biological science. Ancient Irish legend even has it that the greatest of all Irish heroes, the tragic Cuchulain, was conceived after his mother swallowed a Mayfly. A divine paternity! In Ireland anything can suddenly become numinous and wonderful. The fish—the salmon itself—is full of symbolic significance, often of wisdom and knowledge. The poet W. B. Yeats reported that he saw a man on the road at Ross's

Point carrying two salmon, one hanging from each hand. Yeats wondered if it was a man with two souls, or two souls with but a single man between them.

Even the water is holy in Ireland's folklore. "What's water," asked Yeats, "but the generated soul!" It's the basis of that abiding trinity of Water, Mayfly, and Fish, a triune model of a vital synergism that is more than ecological in its applications.

But to get on with the story and out on fabled Lough Corrib for brown trout with our long dapping rods, gossamer "blow" lines of floss, and size 10 dry-fly hooks on which to impale the live dun Drakes, maybe two at a time. It was easy to get a supply of those flies from the enterprising boys waiting to sell to us anglers as we drove through their village on our way to Ned's boat landing.

> Oh, 'tis grand to be out in the grey old boat,
> with a friend and a rod and a fly,
> And to feel the lift of the boat as we drift
> by the shoals where the brown trout lie.

That's the way the old song describes the day we were to have.

Out we went in Ned's old boat, to likely shoals where we let our lines of floss blow down the wind carrying our Mayflies to cruising brown trout, those creatures of the many black spots. We could touch the fly daintily down to the surface just here and now over there with the slightest lift and swing of the long rod, letting the wind do the work—the wind that at any hour might turn to a gale, with, like as not, a lashing rain. But unlike his fair-weather American cousin, our Irish angler prefers the wind and rain and is always ready for it. It's then that his fishing is often at its best.

And if the weather should get too bad, not far off, not too long a row, there's always an inviting island-haven for shelter under a whitethorn bush and lunch at a small fire for the teakettle. As long as there's enough blue overhead to make yourself a shirt, as they say, the weather can't be too terrible.

In any case, everything comes together with a friend, a rod, and a fly. One feels . . . fulfilled, as the Mayfly itself is fulfilling.

But sometimes the fish don't move, and few of them moved that day—perhaps too bright, too dry, too calm a day. So we went to artificials—conventional rods and lines—with no better results. The recalcitrant trout were throwing us back upon conversation, talk that ran to the endless dressings of imitations of the Green Drake and Spent Gnat Mayflies and how none of them enjoys consensus. And then we talked of smoking salmon, of tackle and boats and islands in the Lough, of the weather and the water, of home and of our children— all of it by indirection directly about our friendship. It was a profoundly Irish day.

Win or lose, take fish or no, one always wins when the Mayfly is up. It's enough, more than enough, just to be out there and give oneself over to the lift of the boat; the enchantment of May's grand event, the rebirth of the prince of all flies; and, for a couple of old men at least, the furtive hope that they might see it again, yet one more time, next year: *Go mbeimid beo ag an am seo aris.*

Postscript: I take no little pleasure in the fact that I was able to bring together one of America's greatest anglers and angling theorists, Vincent Marinaro (*A Modern Dry Fly Code* [New York: Putnam, 1950]), and the master of modern angling entomology in the British Isles, J. R. Harris of Dublin (*An Angler's Entomology* [London: Collins, 1952]). After the two old men had thoroughly argued the point in Dublin, Vince returned home proclaiming in his inimitably assured way that the Green Drake Mayfly of Ireland and the Green Drake of Pennsylvania's Penn's Creek were not just similar, but one and the same. And that settled that. At least for me.

Erin's Bluegills

When her father asked her what kind of fish she hoped to catch with her grandfather out in Colorado, Erin, then three, replied as succinctly and clearly as any properly-brought-up Brooklyn girl could that she hoped to catch some "lox-spread" fish.

Not until the following summer, did Erin, by then a year older, and her grandfather—me— at last go after the fish in Shanahan's Pond. This first fishing trip for Erin had to be done right, according to the book, a purist enterprise. Therefore, a couple dozen worms and a neat little black, white, and yellow bobber with a #8 Eagle Claw bait hook made up the tackle—not for lox, but surely for the bluegill waiting there for her. A seven-foot, one-piece glass fly rod was the tool of delivery, just right for the serious and determined little girl.

We got to the pond shortly after ten on a lovely summer morning. We chose a spot on the west side of the pond, got rigged up, and tossed in the first worm—with grandfather's casting help. At once the bobber bobbed. Bobbed and dove, rose again to the surface, and dove again, to Erin's fascination. We set the hook and missed, lost the worm and tried again, with the same results. For Erin it was something utterly, absolutely new, unimagined, even baffling, until on the next worm, the fish got hooked securely and fought hard, with those determined broad-sided stubborn runs typical of bluegill. Obviously—to grandfather—this was no ordinary bluegill.

He was extraordinary—big, thick of shoulder, with that squarishness of profile that big, tough, hoary old bluegill develop. Safely onshore, he had to be adequately admired, photographed, and bagged, this first full pound of a bluegill, before we were back at it again, with another worm sent out to do its duty. Now the action was nearly constant, the fish stealing the worm as often as not, but always there was the fascination of watching the bobber dance and dive enticingly on the water. Any angler who cannot feel the pleasure and excitement of a fish's having commerce with a worm and the transmission of that action to a bobber on the surface is fit to die in a ditch. And that's all there is to it.

Well, Erin caught yet another lunker bluegill, and, almost to stretch belief, another one yet. The three big fellows weighed in at two pounds, three ounces. North of the Mason-Dixon, that's heroic bluegilling. Several more average fish came to the worms before there were no more worms. So we took off for home. Surely Erin's mother and grandmother would be deeply impressed at her prowess.

What was so interesting is that Erin seemed almost at once to catch on to the dynamics of landing the fish. No running in excited abandon up the shore, dragging the fish from the water. She sensed how to make the fish work against the rod until it tired and could be brought to old Grandaddy's hand, where she could examine the fish carefully and see how the worm had fared in the process.

She thought that dropping the bag containing the three big ones on the rocky ground would expedite killing them, something she felt it important to do. Looking at the photographs of Erin with her fish reveals the studious, rather somber mood in which she fished for them. Some kind of private negotiation with life and death was going on deep inside her: the lives of the fish, the worms, the vibrant life of the pond around her— who knows what all she was, as they say now, "processing"?

Back home, grandmother did indeed make much over the fish, realizing clearly that one could fish a lifetime and not catch three such fine bluegill. And when mother arrived to see what had been wrought, she was even more pleased and excited. She at once recalled how she had fished for bluegill back in Pennsylvania and so could understand what an achievement in Big Fish these three sunnies were.

Then they got scaled, lost their heads and guts, and were readied for frying the next day. And delicious they were, too. Not least delectable were the tasty tails fried crisp—always a delicacy in this family.

Erin Ana Reynolds had had her first fishing trip, and it was a success. She disported herself in an exemplary manner. She put good food on her grandmother's table and, one hopes, a memory in her heart of hearts. And the whole thing was indeed done right.

All Four

On a fine autumn afternoon a couple of years back, I drove to a forbidden lake to fling my flies. Not much was happening around the inlet. It took most of an hour to connect with a fine rainbow of about a pound on a #16 Caribou Captain. A beautiful fish. But after that flash in the pan, even less was going on. A nap seemed appropriate, so, in the warm autumn sunshine, in the comfortable grasses, I stretched out and nodded off for maybe half an hour. It was delicious.

I roused to see some fish moving at the surface, maybe fifty feet out. Reorganizing myself, I put a fly over one of them, and it took nicely. This one proved to be a gorgeous brook trout only a little smaller than the rainbow.

The next strike came a hundred yards around the lakeshore. This one was a cutthroat, as much a looker as the brook, and of the same size. By now, I was beginning to think of the possibility of getting "four aces," a grand slam of the four major trout species. I couldn't remember when, if ever, I'd actually accomplished that. Now, here I was, holding three of the aces from the deck and indulging my fantasy of the fourth.

I had only the most tentative relationship with two other fish on my stroll around the lake. A few fish were cruising here and there in a desultory way, sipping from the surface and moving on. Unable to intercept any of them, I decided to pitch my dry out about forty feet and just let it sit there until some cruiser came by and took a look at it.

I waited a good fifteen or twenty minutes—forever when it comes to still-fishing a dry fly on a lake. I even sat down a while.

Then it happened. A fish came by, took a look, liked what it saw, and hit. The trout put on a fine show, complete with two tail dances, and dared me to think that it might just be a brown, my ace of spades, completing my four-of-a-kind, the hand that takes all pots. And it was. One! Two! Three! Four!

The satisfaction was deep. I only wish that I could have seen all four laid out side by side, each at the moment of its capture. How lovely they would have been together. How many anglers have ever seen precisely that sight—all four trout at once, in the moment of their living perfection? Few, I'll bet. As it was, I released them, each to appear again another day.

Surely that was enough. I quit and headed for home. A limit must be placed, after all, not only on fish but even on pleasure.

The Boy in the White

After Wordsworth

At twilight, looking for rising fish from a bridge over the White River in western Colorado, I noticed a solitary boy, maybe thirteen, stash his fishing rod and shirt in the river rocks, and, silhouetted against the evening sky, pick up a piece of driftwood maybe as thick as your wrist and as long as your arm. He threw that stick as far upriver as he could into the deep and dangerous current and, calculating just the right moment, dove in headlong to swim out, grab the stick, and breast the current to the other bank. Immediately, he threw the stick back in again, and again swam the powerful river for it—just as a dog fetches a stick thrown by its master. Over and over that boy swam for his stick with unself-conscious abandon. He seemed at once to possess the river and his own life.

Today, I wonder in what merciless ways, as his years roll on, the doors of that boy's prison house will close on him. Or will he somehow find a way to trail behind him the glory of his river?

All I know is that in the rivers I've waded, I've never known the courage nor the strength nor the freedom of that boy, challenging himself in the White River twilight. I won't forget him.

Thinking About It

Let the Reader Beware

The wary reader may sense what appears to be a disconformity of thought and feeling about nature and anglers in three or four of the following essays. I've puzzled over the difficulty and might well have taken those essays in hand and forced them into conformity with one another. I might have rescued their themes-in-common and discarded the rest as spurious.

Instead, I've decided to let them stand, in the belief that their possible contradictions more truly represent not only my thinking but the complexities of fly fishing itself at the beginning of this new millennium. The issue of the human being in, of, and against nature is relentlessly a vexing one.

Fishing the Depths
or
Why Do We Do It?

In his cursory critical survey of the literature of fly fishing *Haunted by Waters* (Athens, Ohio: Ohio University Press, 1998), Mark Browning calls attention to the fact that from the great *Treatyse* of 1496 through Walton's *Compleat Angler* in 1653,

British trouting ethos insisted upon the enrichment of the angler's inner spirit and an intimate and varied experience of the natural world around him.

After Walton, however, a radical change took place. Setting aside any notion of a soulful appreciation of nature as the mark of successful fishing, British angling literature, down to the present day, has insisted upon location, technique, tactics, and tackle—all that would help kill ever more, ever bigger trout and salmon.

We learn that it is in America that the Walton tradition has continued unabated and that American writers on angling have generally insisted that there is a great deal more to fishing than catching fish. They embrace the subjective, the emotional, the rhapsodic in both fishing and nature.

Contemporary American writers on fly fishing are of a single voice: that the angler luring a trout from the depths to an artificial fly ought to be in effective reciprocity with the whole of nature. This, they suggest, can raise the angler to a state of spiritual privilege. We learn this in often tormented rhetoric reaching for the authority of the poetic in order to codify a high and mysterious process.

These writers, turning the full force of their inveterate American habit of introspection onto fly fishing, extend their idea of oneness with nature to include Sunday-supplement, New Age psychologizing about "fishing up the Self" out of primal waters as a way of understanding ourselves and why we fish. If those discussions are frequently at loose ends or overwrought, the hardheaded substance of the theory goes like this: we are instructed by psychoanalytic theory that the Self is an archetype lodged in the unconscious. That archetype is mysteriously expressed in dream, myth, and art, and employs maternal imagery. In the Unconscious, with its immense, containing maternal energies, the fetal self seeks to break loose to fulfillment, to free itself from the binding and dangerous mother-matrix into an effective, independent personhood.

The theory teaches that this effort, or adventure, of the Self is the way of the hero to fully integrated human life. And what is so interesting is that the symbolism of waters, of fish and fishing, is a vehicle for this archetype of the Self to break through to consciousness. We learn that wherever we throw a line or cast a net, there lies not only the fish that's provender to nourish the body, but also the Self, all on the same hook.

It's a compelling concept; it explains a great deal about many things. I've been much drawn to it for a long time. But now I've come to believe that it's too extravagant an idea to fit the daily experience of our angling. It's not the sort of consciousness we take with us to the stream. Discussions of this "fishing for the Self" become pretentious and striving for effect. They tend to develop a mysticism around angling and promise too much from it. They foster a certain "we few, we happy few" mentality.

So, what *can* we say about why we fish? What can we say that we all can live with and believe in? With the pressures mounting against blood sports, it's increasingly important that we say something effective and articulate about the values we find in our fishing, something useful about why we do it.

There's a way, I think, not altogether unrelated to the fishing-up-the-Self idea, of explaining why it is that we fish. For me it has to do with identity, the personal, workaday identity that I claim for myself. All of us in earnest about our lives want to know that deep down we are this or that. We sense that whatever "it" is, we must be "it" as resolutely as we can, follow the "Here I stand" position nailed to the doors of our public and private personae.

To identify oneself as a serious fisherman is a seriously active stance. Our sport is anything but passive, anything but merely diverting, relaxing, or time-killing. Anything but a hobby. My own fishing is, in fact, so active that it's downright aggressive—in spirit if no longer, alas, in (aging) body.

I think that I've been two things in my public life: a fisherman and a teacher. I'm not sure which encompasses the other, but I suspect that it's the angler. Whenever my colleagues wanted to know what sort of beast I was, I always tried to convey that I was an angler, one with that special slant on things.

What I do as that angler is re-create myself over and over on the stream (as I do in these words). That is, I re-identify, re-energize myself. At no time do I feel more myself, more the way I want to feel, than just before, during, and after fishing.

My fishing is never, as some aver, passive recreation or mere hobby. It has become something of a way of life. Paul Schullery has said that "calling fishing a hobby is like calling brain surgery a job." And he ought to know.

Farmers, hunters and fishermen, priests and healers, cooks, bakers and builders, singers and storytellers all made up that first company, that first great guild of workers, upon which humankind came to depend. Note that we anglers are squarely enrolled in that immemorial guild. In our sport, transforming work into play, we memorialize that essential labor.

It's serious business, this fishing, whether we haul nets in the North Sea for herring or throw tiny dry flies at sophisticated trout in a spring creek. Fishing is everywhere, in every way, the same thing. We practice our ancient productive craft confident of its ancient unity and importance.

But we must not suggest that fishing alone is so highly important, much less exclusively essential, in the processes of self-identification. We uppity fly fishermen in particular should be more modest and restrained. We must remember that there's more than one way to shape a psyche, a persona.

Without appealing for democracy among anglers and their philosophies, I think that we must calm down a bit and allow that there are ways other than fishing for people to find and develop a fully integrated self and to declare an identity. Why should not a baker find the same sort of intense, even joyous affirmation of identity in the work of his or her hands? Everyone must be able to come into the Kingdom.

Fishing to enhance the sense of a particular identity, to feel more intensely the person we want to be, is not so rapturous a claim as fishing the Unconscious for what may be after all only a generic and mythic Self. But affirming an identity, a persona, on the stream is a modest and workable idea—comprehensible to and possible for all anglers, whether of fly, bait, or spoon. It's reward and justification enough for our devotion to our sport and a heavy enough stick with which to beat off those who think only in terms of hobbies and casual recreation. It may not satisfy those who would eliminate all blood sports, but it can keep us proud in the face of their hysteria.

When we have said all this about why we fish in the first place, we can turn to reasons why some of us insist on casting flies most or all of the time. I think it becomes fairly easy to explain—with lots of good reasons, not the least of which is the fact that it's easier to tie flies than to dig worms.

Though I fish almost exclusively with flies, I feel strongly that I must see myself first simply as a fisherman, then as a fly fisher. Fly fishing should emerge as but one way, albeit a splendid way, among the vast number of ways of taking fish. The proud claim to have been always and only a fly fisher rings false for me.

If, as I said, it's easy to understand why we may dedicate ourselves to fly fishing, let me put myself to the test, as I close, by listing a dozen reasons for doing so:

Fly fishing is elegant and graceful.
Fly-fishing tackle is handsome and simple, yet complex.
Fly fishing is much about handcraftsmanship.
Artificial flies are highly interesting in their own right.
Fly-fishing entomology is sometimes as fascinating as fishing.
Fly fishing usually takes place in attractive natural surroundings.
Fly-fishing tradition and literature are rich and rewarding.

Fly fishing can be enjoyed throughout one's life.
Fly fishing encourages an active imagination.
Fly fishing is companionable.
Fly fishing is highly pleasurable to think about.
Fly fishing is often the most productive method of fishing.

There may be more, but surely these are reasons enough.

Postscript: I recently saw Tom Stoppard's new play, *The Invention of Love.* In it, three Oxford undergraduates of the 1880s are out on the river, lazing about on a small island. Conversation turns on the plaintive fact that one of them has never kissed a girl. He wonders what it must be like. Another of the young scholars replies that it's like the third thing when you thought there were only two. I wonder if fishing the fly isn't a bit like that: the third thing when we thought there were only two.

Stoppard, in addition to being one of the world's great playwrights, is an advanced fly fisherman, with half a mile of the Kennet in Hampshire—or at least he had it when his dear friend the illustrious actor Michael Hodern still lived. They fished it together. The Kennet? The Kennet is the third English chalk stream when you thought there were only two: the Test and the Itchen.

On Pilgrimage

During the Age of Faith, untold numbers of people made springtime pilgrimage to the great shrines of their faith, the most popular of which were in England and Spain. In Spain they went to view the relics of the Apostle James in his cathedral church at Compostela. The pilgrim needed only look overhead at the night sky and follow the Milky Way, the "Road of St. James," straight on to the relics of the saint.

Or pilgrims could travel southeast out of London, along the April way of Chaucer's company to Canterbury, to the great cathedral church where sycophant knights of Henry II murdered Archbishop Thomas à Becket on Christmas Eve 1170 and made him a saint and martyr. Countless pilgrims made their way to this most famous of shrines to be blessed and view the fragment of Becket's sword-hewn skull.

For anglers, a faithful lot if there ever was one, the road of pilgrimage is to the River Dove in Derbyshire, England's north country, to the spot on that river where Charles Cotton built the seventeenth-century, rustic baroque Fishing House for his mentor and fatherly friend, Izaak Walton. Though tucked away on private property, it can be closely approached to where the brave of heart can sneak in for a look. Whoever fishes trout, salmon, or grayling ought to come as close as possible to this small stone shrine with the affecting insignia above the door:

The Fishing House

E·H·N·

IWCC
Piscatoribus Sacrum 1674

Walton cherished the Dove, though in those days it was a long, hard trip away from his home in London, where he fished the nearby Lea. The Dove is a freestone river of both rugged and serene beauty and sacred to the memory of Cotton, whose chapter on fly fishing in Walton's *Compleat Angler* represents the beginning of modern fly fishing, and Walton himself, who so richly defined the temperament of angling and described its experience.

But if we can't make our way to England, to Derbyshire, the Dove, and this famous fishing hut, perhaps a fair exchange might be a pilgrimage to the fishing hut overlooking the fly-casting ponds in Golden Gate Park in San Francisco. Built in the 1930s in the American rustic style by the City of San Francisco with funding from the New Deal Works Progress Administration under Franklin Roosevelt, the hut and ponds in this secluded corner of the beautiful park stand in testament to the imagination of a great city and the WPA at a time of creative and generous political consciousness that seems alien in America today.

The several concrete ponds are shallow, built for tournament casting and casting games "back then," when a long cast was eighty feet. On a gentle slope above the ponds sits the handsome hut. Rough, ready, and surprisingly dark inside, it's lined with lockers in which members of the Golden Gate Casting Club can stash their gear, and benches on which to do whatever one does in a fishing hut. It was these San Francisco anglers who in the fifties and sixties so revolutionized fly casting. Finally the dynamics of the fly in the air, for our time, were mastered.

Not to be missed, in the rough-hewn door of this fabulous hut, is a stained-glass roundel some fifteen inches in diameter, depicting a Royal Coachman. I suppose that in this day when anything and everything can find its way into the worst clichés of hobbyist stained glass, a depiction of a Royal Coachman is no longer remarkable or spectacular. Ah, but to enter the hut, almost as into a camera obscura, and there from the dark and dusky interior see this brilliant glass Royal Coachman illuminated by western light from over the Pacific . . . for us pilgrims, the experience is inimitable.

Back in the sixties, feeling a little pilgrimish myself, I was able to drive up from Palo Alto on several Sunday mornings to cast on these ponds, struggling hard to toss a fly eighty feet. There I was one morning, using my big eight-and-a-half-foot, five-strip cane rod with a #9 line, doing my best, when a man sidled up to me—a club member, I assumed. He remarked briefly on my rod, asking if he might try it. Sure. He took the rod, planted his feet with care, made a single false cast, double-hauled (right there on these ponds where the double-haul was conceived), and sent that fly clear across the water and into the shrubbery beyond. I watched unbelieving as that narrow loop of line seemed to climb up and up into the sky before turning over and dropping the fly back to earth. "Nice rod," he said, handing it back. "That's 130 feet." And walked away. I was thrilled and humbled all in a moment. It was a miracle of sorts, like encountering the resident saint of the place, and in the flesh—which is exactly what one hopes for on a pilgrimage.

Toward an Idea of Water

Extracts

After the manner of Herman Melville in *Moby Dick*

All day we've faced the barren wastes
Without a taste of water,

Cool clear water.
Old Dan and I with throats burned dry
And souls that cry for water,
Cool clear water.

—*Sons of the Pioneers*

In the beginning God created the heavens and the earth. And the earth was waste and void; and darkness was upon the face of the deep: and the spirit of God moved upon the face of the waters.

—*Genesis 1:2*

As the hart panteth after the water brooks,
So panteth my soul after thee, O God.

—*Psalm 42*

And thou shalt be like a watered garden, and like a spring of water, whose waters fail not.

—*Isaiah 58:11*

They have forsaken me the fountain of living water, and hewed them out cisterns, broken cisterns, that can hold no water.

—*Jeremiah 2:13*

St. John likens our proper spiritual condition to "rivers of living water."
Living fountains of water

—*Revelation 7:17*

The fountain of the water of life

—*Revelation 21:6*

False as water!

—*Shakespeare, Othello, Act V*

Soul of man, how like water thou art!

—*J. W. von Goethe*

Take almost any path you please, and ten to one it carries you down in a dale, and leaves you there by a pool in the stream. There is magic in it. . . . Yes, as everyone knows, meditation and water are wedded forever.

—*Herman Melville, Moby Dick*

What's water but the generated soul?

—*W. B. Yeats*

No matter what they say, it's the water that gives you gas.

—*Countess Aurelia in Giradoux's*
The Madwoman of Chaillot

And, from the Meditations of Piscator

Our mothers created us from the waters of our watersheds. We are born of the water.

The fish we pursue continually test it.

Scientists now teach us that water is the one essential in the universe for life to occur. Water appears to be the Big Secret.

The ancients taught that sources of water were sacred. The Industrial Revolution taught us that water was a vehicle to dissolve and carry away our wastes.

There is no new water on the planet. We use and reuse the primordial supply countless times over.

We only borrow water from the great reservoir system of the planet and depend on it for our ultimate economy.

Without that water, there could be no agriculture, no commerce, no culture, no human community, no purification.

Why then, do we abuse the rivers of living water on which our lives and spirits depend?

The Blues of It

More than sixty years of fishing. Once in a while I get the blues of it. I wonder why I do it, have done it, and will keep on doing it.

For instance, why should what I did with such zeal at thirteen still compel me at seventy-five? Am I in any significant way, other than in my genetics, the same person I was back then? They tell me that by now, all the cells in my body have been replaced many times over. And my life experiences could readily have sent me off in directions leading me far from fishing.

But for all that, the fact is that I started to get serious about life through my fascination with fishing—and opera—and have remained that way.

My preoccupation with fishing, and with the opera, music, and theatre in general, served to attract the attention of grown-ups and elicit their approval. I was taken more seriously as a kid than I would have had I been interested, say, only in automobiles. Fishing and the opera—the opera!— what do you make of a kid like that?

I think that fishing gave me a way to be known, an identity of sorts. And being known is profoundly important to anyone's life. In my case, it was satisfying to be known as a fisherman.

My father neither fished nor hunted. At home I was encouraged passively, but my fishing and hunting got me into a gang of six other high-school lads with whom I was to have the finest of associations, enduring to this day. We hammered out identities over the poker table, with our new tobacco pipes, our fishing and hunting, and the endless debate over which was the greater music: Roy Acuff's "Wabash Cannonball" or the overture to Wagner's *Tannhäuser*. The recordings alternated endlessly on the old Victrola as we played our cards, night after night.

In this way we laid down the foundations of our personalities—our characters. And, it was a grand opportunity for me to play the snob—a role that came all too naturally. I fed on what I thought, and still think, was the elegance of fishing. It became an aesthetic as much as a sport. I saw no real conflict in sensibility between fishing and Wagner. I could cock a snoot in support of either.

Angling can be quite sophisticated. That sophistication lies in its contemplative nature. Surely angling is the most "thought-full" of all sports. Fishing is engaging even when one is not actually fishing. It is an idea, a subject, to carry about and work over endlessly, anywhere, anytime, supported, as it is, by its literature, finer and more extensive than that of any other sport.

Then, too, our fishing tends to develop right along with us. We sense from the start that its possibilities are inexhaustible, and so it sustains us, challenges us, sticks with us throughout the years. Fishing also has the wonderful virtue of accommodating to our ever declining physical powers. A frail old man probably can't play tennis, but he still can fish.

Why, then, should I ever get the blues of it? Let me count the ways:

Catch-and-release trout fishing may fairly be said to have saved trout fishing in our time, what with the vastly increasing number of anglers beating our waters nearly to death. But catch-and-release is in the last analysis a phony way of fishing and a degrading thing to do to a trout: abusing the poor creature for our pleasure. When fishing is no longer a means of procuring food, the risk of mannerism and decadence comes racing in. It may be necessary, this no-kill policy, but it can give you the blues. Think, that the climactic moment of landing a fish is too often a grotesque fumbling around trying to extract a hook; it's downright distressful, and always hard on the fish. We have come to enjoy "long-line releases." It might have been better to stay home.

The crowds of fishermen themselves can be deeply depressing. Finding a place to piss is more and more a problem—especially dire for women—as so many of our waters have become suburban. Solitude on the stream is now almost impossible. Competition for the water is keen and often runs rude-to-hostile.

The solution to crowding—privatization—is as bad as the problem itself. More and more, quality fishing must be purchased on private property. The public is increasingly shut out in betrayal of what for better or worse has been the American ideal of sport: free public access. The irony is that we now see members of the public themselves banding together in associations to privatize water for their exclusive use. "If you can't beat 'em, join 'em," as the saying goes.

Part and parcel of catch-and-release is the intense and successful management that fishing has come under. Biologists and managers have saved the day, no doubt about it. But the downside of all that is the artificiality, lack of spontaneity, and denaturing, the control that always threatens to become control for its own sake. Fishing just isn't natural any longer, nor are we, the anglers. We might almost as well be fishing on a golf course.

Perhaps a metaphor for this development is the presence of Whirling Disease in our streams, an affliction that can destroy wholesale entire generations of infant trout—*Myxobolis cerebralis,* that most clever of parasites, visited on us like a scourge made possible by the very civilization on which we so miserably depend. And to think that our very wading shoes may be carrying the parasite, this plague, from stream to stream. And that anglers, upon leaving a stream, may one day be forced to wade through a disinfecting tank in order to prevent the contagion from spreading elsewhere. We may as well have our waders splashed with a blood-red cross to mark the presence of plague.

Furthermore, "commodification," the working of something into salable form and then flogging it mercilessly, compromises the development that even fishing has undergone in the last three decades. Fishing becomes commodity; everything becomes commodity.[11] Even the U.S. Forest Service, having swallowed the sugared pill of its own folly, now speaks of the people it serves as "customers," failing to realize that its rangers must then become "salesmen." One should have a very long spoon when one eats with *this* Devil.

Many of us today lack the individuality, not to mention the traditional eccentricity, necessary to protect us from commodification, exploitation in the marketplace. Technology has squeezed us into a box, pressured us into conformity; we express not our individual selves but the images concocted in catalogues. We have been objectified, turned into a market.

Time was when angling was not fashionable, not something that smart young people wanted to be caught doing. Fishing was thought to require nothing more than patience, by which was meant the ability merely to watch a bobber bob. But now look at us: regiments of superbly equipped, well-trained, single-minded, impatient, identical seekers after trout. And up to the very snuff of fashion into the bargain.

Not long ago I talked with Bud Lilly, the grand old man of Montana trouting, who said that he thought there must be intense regulation of our great rivers, that there will soon come a time when a day's fishing on the Madison will be possible only by winning a state-run lottery. Lilly went on to say that he believed intense "social control" (his words) will be necessary if fishing as we know it, or want to know it, is to survive. I flinched at the term "social control." It points, it seems, directly to the ultimate denaturing of angling.

And in my gloom I recall the words of the legendary Vincent Marinaro, who said, on our way to Pennsylvania's Letort back on a beautiful Sunday morning in 1973, that he believed trout fishing to be ultimately incompatible with modern civilization. If part of the legacy of the modern last century is that it did in trout fishing, what may we now expect from the postmodern millennium into which we have stumbled headlong?

It's thinking like this that gives me the blues and makes me wonder sometimes if it was worth mastering the blood knot all those years ago.

The Politics of It

The politics of salmonids, and their sustaining waters, is grim, uphill work. The politics of the Old Right threaten environmental policy through dedication to special interests and resource exploitation. And the Left, that should-be protector and nourisher of the environment and its creatures, has been usurped by a new breed, a coalition of activists intent upon exposing the failures, if not the evils, they believe endemic to the Western cultural/political experience. This new breed appears now to dominate our intellectual streets.

Conservation as we once we knew it is eclipsed by a radical environmentalism, the creed of a new generation of social critics, who, coming of intellectual age in America during the darkness of the latter third of the twentieth century, see human beings—especially human beings in the Western democracies—as guilty of the Rape of Nature, to say nothing of the oppression of native peoples. Ordinary, well-meaning people are the evil in this equation of the new "environmentalism."

And so, traditional, progressive conservation efforts are radically decentered. The decades of hard work on behalf of the environment by hunters and fishermen in cooperation with progressive government policy and a fast-awakening public is now in serious trouble. Good causes like environmentalism get into the hands of excessive people, like the animal-rights groups, who look on hunters and fishers as little better than wanton murderers. These new critics, despising hunters and fishers of the "developed" world particularly, would exclude these enemies of nature from a rightful and integral role in it. They believe that, given their way, nature can somehow be purified. "Nativism", "new tribalism," and "multiculturalism" are some of the watchwords. The politically correct opposition to "exotic" brown, rainbow, and brook trout in Colorado waters is a mark of how subtle and insidious the argument has become.

The traditional Right worsens the situation by regarding government effort on behalf of the environment and the public interest as no better than a thievery of private interests and that personal liberty limited to private property.

Nonprofit organizations like Trout Unlimited are nickled and dimed to death by having to oppose one piece after another of nefarious legislation from the Right, prevented as they are by their charters from going after the real culprit— political party policy itself and the privilege that the now compromised ballot box can give it. What these well-intended organizations can do about the powerful cultural, intellectual forces of the Left and Right, at work to radicalize environmental issues in their own image and beyond all recognition, is even more problematic and discouraging.

Meditating on a Meditation

Perhaps the greatest of all studies on hunting is Spanish philosopher Jose Ortega y Gasset's *Meditations on Hunting* (1972). Ortega takes us deeper into the mind and spirit of the hunter and the hunted than any other writer. I read him at just the right moment, when I was wondering about the ethics of the hunt and my relationship to it. Ortega cleared my head. At the same time, he troubled me deeply by his few and only passing references to fishing.

Ortega writes:

> About 1938, Jules Romains, a hardened writer of the Front Populaire, published an article venting his irritation with the workers, because they, having gained a tremendous reduction in the work day and being in possession of long idle hours, had not learned to occupy themselves other than in the most uncouth form of hunting: fishing with a rod, the favorite sport of the good French bourgeois. The ill-humored writer was deeply irritated that a serious revolution had been achieved with no apparent result other than that of augmenting the number of rod fishermen.[12]

Romains—a leading French intellectual, playwright, poet, and radical of the Left—just the sort that I ought to take most seriously and credit most readily, said this! And here, after he takes the unusual step of locating angling as a branch of hunting, declares it the most "uncouth" form of hunting to boot. What am I to think? What can I make of this scathing denigration of what is so dear to me?

Of course, I have clearly in mind the conventional image of the solitary Parisian fisherman, sitting there motionless on the Seine for endless hours with never so much as a bite. Is this the fisherman of Romains's indictment? Perhaps. But still I wonder if there really may be something inherently inferior about fishing when contrasted with hunting larger, land-dwelling animals.

I was struck by Ortega's remarkable discussion of how in the process of our social evolution we have found that oppressive, spirit-dulling, time-destroying work takes from us what Ibsen called the "joy of life." Ortega speaks of how aristocrats—those liberated from the drudgery of daily subsistence work—chose to fill their days to cultivate that joy: "Now this greatly liberated man, the aristocrat, has always done the same things: raced horses, or competed in physical exercises, gathered at parties, the feature of which is usually dancing, and [engaging] in conversation. But before any of those, and consistently more important than all of them has been . . . hunting."[13]

He goes on to make hunting the primary diversion of nobles and kings, but notes that all of the social classes have wanted the same privileged activity and that we can therefore "divide the felicitous occupations of the normal man into four categories: hunting, dancing, racing, and conversing."[14]

Romains would consign rod fishermen to the bottom of the heap of hunters. Why? Is it the absence of risk, of danger, in fishing that lowers it in the general esteem? Is it what many people imagine as the sedentary character of fishing that diminishes it? Is fishing too passive? Not wild enough? Could fish be too far removed from us for them to be worthy opponents in the life-and-death struggle of hunting?

Izaak Walton characterized angling as "the contemplative man's recreation." Ortega characterized the hunter as the human being at maximum alert in his contest with a worthy animal adversary, only a little less worthy than himself. And so, would it be fair to say that fishing focuses the reflective angler more gently inward, whereas more conventional hunting focuses the violent hunter outward into the exciting world of life-and-death contest? If angling is contemplation, may it not sometimes result in a lassitude that actually dulls the spirit?

In my meditations I reflect on my contentment and pleasure in fishing close to home, here along Colorado's Front Range. Am I too content? Ought I to be braving more, pushing further and harder? Does my easy acceptance of the comforts of home suggest a spiritual complaisance or lethargy, the sort that earned Romains's bitter criticism of rod fishermen, the least of the hunters?

On Killing Trout

I believe in catch-and-release. I believe in no-kill, and gladly. I know that without catch-and-release in fish management, there would be little quality angling anywhere, except, perhaps, in big reservoirs. So, again I say, I believe in catch-and-release . . . mostly, that is.

And that qualifying word *mostly* makes all the difference. It keeps alive what I understand to be the essential truth and spirit of fishing—in spite of the degradation that I believe superintense management and development have wrought on today's fish and fisher. Let me explain.

I believe that we must always remember, and keep alive in our consciousness, that fishing is a way of providing food for sustenance. That angling as a sport, a recreation, is a comparatively new development in human history, and angling's transformation into sport is not ultimately essential to it. We need occasionally to kill a fish in recognition of what it is to fish. We need to remind ourselves that the supermarket as primary source of our daily bread is far removed from the days when that bread came directly from the work of our own hands or not at all.

We ought to practice catch-and-release with both enthusiasm and regret—enthusiasm for the increased size and numbers of trout generally available to our rods, and regret for the increasingly artificial, developed conditions of our fishing.

Not only that, but the fish are due an apology for what we do to them. Mustn't we agree that it is probably a morally superior act to kill and eat a fish than it is to use it—abuse it—only for our pleasure and diversion? For me the use of that commercially available stomach pump instead of the sharp-bladed knife to determine what a trout is eating is the ultimate in abuse and violation. Think of that pump for a moment as an instrument of rape, an implement designed only to satisfy our curiosity, at our pleasure. For me, angling that would approve a device like this has become decadent. And I'm shocked when I read of its being used by those who should know better.

There is no way, I feel, that we can deny that ours is a blood sport. We must accept that fact and make the best we can of it. We willingly kill our fellow creatures. To instill the no-kill idea too early and too rigorously in a child learning to fish is seriously to distort that initial experience. There can be no truth in fishing for the young angler who does not know the blood of a fish on his or her hands, nor the presence of that fish on the family table. It's a matter of facing reality, of knowing what it is that we do out there on the stream. We should recall how the argument against hunting that promoted the use of camera instead of gun never really took hold. Hunters knew in their bowels that the camera was not, and never could be, a substitute for the bow or gun. Hunting is, after all and at bottom, a means of putting food on the table—or it ought to be.

All killing should be carefully restrained within the bounds of enlightened stewardship, within the imperatives of the new consciousness, the new cultural paradigms, that appear to be developing. We should shoot only a minimum bag. We should kill only a few symbolic fish. But we should with some regularity re-enact that ceremony of the kill and its provision of life-sustaining food. The ceremony can help keep us in touch with the tragic human fix, preserve us from the dangers of sentimentality, and the softening of the moral brain.

Remember the Old Man's apology to the giant marlin in Hemingway's *The Old Man and the Sea*? "Fish," he said, "I love you and respect you very much. But I will kill you dead before this day ends."[15]

And so we kill in desire, sorrow, and love—just as, in fact, we live and die. That's what I mean by the "tragic human fix." It's recognition and acceptance of this that I'm holding out for.

Lee Wulff wrote—and is forever quoted and misquoted on it—that a trout is too valuable to be caught only once. That's not altogether true. There are catches so extraordinary, so life-enhancing, so full of symbolic value—for instance, a boy or girl's first trout—that sacrifice of that trout's life is a higher good than its release to what in any case must be another and certain death. It's the genius of humankind that we can transform our necessary life into play. But to play with other creatures from a position of power and control is dangerous indeed. We ought not, then, to play with fish.

We cannot escape, ought not to escape, the dark side of our sport. I can't recommend highly enough the 1993 book *Rivers of Memory* by the late Harry Middleton. Middleton strikes home when he writes "that not everything about fishing is noble and reasonable and sane. That fishing is not an escape from life, but often a deeper immersion into it, all of it, the good and the awful, the joyous and the miserable, the comic, the embarrassing, the tragic, and the sorrowful."[16]

In this golden age of fishing the fly for trout, we ought not to allow our sensibilities to be denied the fullest experience of angling by too technical, overly developed, fastidious, and frenzied a purism. We should never fail to recognize the lurking threat of decadence, all the while thinking that it's really our interest in the refinement of our tackle and methods—as well as conservation—that drives us. We need occasional, memorable moments of bloody hands, of worms and grasshoppers, of minnows and spoons: the whole marvelous range of what fishing so powerfully entails.

I end with the suggestion that if we are breeding, protecting, and nurturing trout exclusively for our pleasure and recreation, only to abuse them through catch-and-release programs—if that's what our fishing in this latter day has become—then we are the trout's worst enemy.

Rather, we ought to square up and kill a trout now and again in the spirit of the Old Man's apology and sorrow, in recognition of the tragedy of life and death that we share with the fish.

It's a terrible problem with no easy answers. No-kill arises from our desperate need to salvage what's left of the quality of our fishing lives on this exquisite but threatened planet. Sadly enough, it may well be too late. But we have to work at it nevertheless, and I suppose that any stab at a solution must involve a personal adjustment as well as a public effort.

In my own case, I killed the first trout I ever caught, and I hope I shall be able to recognize that final transforming moment when it comes, as it must, and kill my last trout.

On the other hand, I shall perhaps want to release that fish to its continuing life, doing for the trout what, in our tragic fix, I cannot do for myself.

Uppercase Nature

I must gird up my loins and admit what many will think rank heresy. It is my strong suspicion that when anglers are at their work, they're not as aware of the wonders and beauties of capital-letter Nature as one might like to believe. Communing with Nature, being sensitive to her ever changing charms and spectacles, may chance to happen from time to time as we fish, but it is not the center of the angling experience that Izaak Walton, four centuries ago, averred that it ought to be.

Embracing Walton's ideal, writers urge us to get in tune with the natural world around us. We're assured that catching fish is not really what's important—what counts is "being at one with Nature." It's an idea hard to resist, yet equally hard to accept when the tone of the argument becomes so effusive and heated.

Few fishing writers today are able to set down more than a few paragraphs without waxing eloquent on the wonders and beauties of Nature. Their enthusiasm runs so high that we begin to feel there must be something wrong with us if we can't match the elevation of their sensibility. I'm cynical enough to think that their paeans to Nature are often only reflexive, a padding out of an essay in ways obligatory to writing about the great out-of-doors.

Years ago, I taught the English Romantic poets to Wyoming ranch kids and oil-field offspring. They had little patience with the great

Romantic tradition of Nature writing. Those young people knew firsthand that Nature was not easy and comforting, as it is so often represented in Romantic literature. Rather, it was serious business, sometimes dangerous, and requiring skilled survival techniques. However splendid that Nature of theirs might be at times, Nature, for them, was an adversary.

Fishing hard requires concentration. When I'm fishing, I'm aware of little else. I'm seldom aware of the enchantments of Nature that Walton encouraged me to cultivate. I can't see them, what with my single-minded attention to fly, water, and trout. Of course, when the spell is broken, when I draw back and look around, I may indeed spot a crop of wild grapes, a superbly sculpted canyon wall, or a kingfisher flashing up the river. But that comes mostly après-fishing, when I move on to other and more varied impressions and ideas, when I relax. Perhaps our pleasures in Nature are akin to Wordsworth's after all, as in his definition of poetry as "emotion recollected in tranquillity." It's not so much that I always experience the pleasures of Nature as that I remember them after the fact, remember the sensations of delight and inspiration etched or plowed subliminally deep into memory.

I've never thought that fishing was relaxing or an act of communion. On the contrary, I've experienced it as an act of studied aggression, an attempt to enter into a different and mysterious realm of existence where I am alien and without rights, yet drawn by powerful forces that I only partly understand.

If I'm after pheasants with loads of 6's, the pheasant and I are in the same realm, breathing the same air, feet touching the same ground. In a sense we understand each other. We play the same game of the chase together. But fishing is different. We go where we don't belong, uninvited and ill prepared. Our fishing methods and tools, after centuries of development, remain crude. We know and understand little about how a trout lives. So it's little wonder that fishing requires such intensity of concentration, such expenditure of psychological, even intellectual, energy to do well. Even then, we often fail utterly.

If that concentration and application cannot be called relaxing, let alone a communion with Nature, if it's not the easy bucolic, pastoral, lyrical pursuit of Father Izaak's ideal, I believe that we can nevertheless claim that it is restorative and re-creative. Going into that other realm—or trying to—takes us so far from our own daily life, its pressures, its sameness and regularities and torments, that we do feel somehow remade in a new way. It's an intense sensation, born of the concentration that allows us to penetrate, to some small extent, the barriers that separate us from that rising trout. We feel strangely new and alive. And that can be marvelous.

(But there I go, doing the very thing I've been railing about—calling down from on high the ineffabilities of Nature. It's hard to avoid.)

Years ago, a student of mine from the Bronx got me talking about a ruffed-grouse hunt I'd been on in the mountains of Pennsylvania. I remember describing the difficulty of walking along the steep, snow-covered, hemlocked mountainsides. I spoke of how placing each step required a new and careful decision. To do otherwise was to risk a bad fall.

Phillip wanted to know why anyone would want to undertake such a thing. I could tell him only that such intensity of concentration and application was strangely energizing, exhilarating. It felt purposeful but resembled relaxation and communion with Nature not at all. The last thing I was aware of was the beauty of the sky overhead, or any of the other natural dainties of the way. I was tuned absolutely and exclusively to staying on my feet in that difficult terrain—and keeping alert to the possible explosion of a grouse underfoot. It was both exhausting and superbly invigorating. I think he understood.

And so I wish that angling writers would stop telling me how in tune they are with Nature when they fish, how wonderful it is just to be out there in it, regardless of how good the fishing is. I don't altogether believe them. They have been inculturated by the Waltonian angling tradition (which, make no mistake, I deeply respect and count myself part of), as well as the fashionable New Age enthusiasms for Nature abundant today. I think that *they* think this is how they ought to feel. And so ought we in turn. But it's a grave danger to pretend to feel what we do not. It's one of the perils of Romantic excess and ill suited to the rougher, tougher, American experience of nature (lowercase now), which has been more contention and danger than symbiosis. I would like to see that capital letter stay off that word, as a start on the way toward emotional candor and balance.

I depart this argument with the observation that if the tender experience of the beauties of Nature were a criterion for successful fishing trips, we would never go to many of the unlovely, unnatural places so popular with anglers today.

Furthermore, we would make sure that all the places we fish were better and more lovingly kept and that principalities and powers could no longer lay them waste.

Look at that Line Hand!

Years ago, I was caught up in the art and ideas of the Middle Ages (as well as angling), and came across this thirteenth-century French drawing in

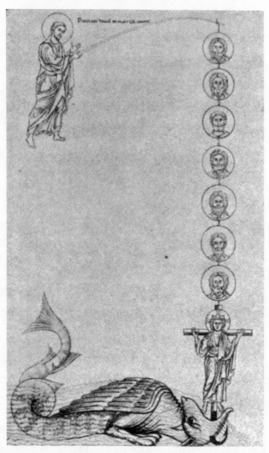

Emile Mâle's *The Gothic Image*.[17] For me, this image of God as angler from the *Hortus Deliciarum,* famous manuscript of the Abbess Herrade, is remarkable for a number of reasons. But first, listen to Honorius of Autun explain the basic iconography: "Leviathan the monster who swims in the sea of the world, is Satan. God threw the line into the sea. The cord of the line is the human descent of Christ, the bait is His divinity. Attracted by the smell of the flesh Leviathan tries to seize it, but the hook tears his jaws."

This miniature from the abbess's manuscript is unusual in its genre in that the fishing line incorporates medallioned heads of the kings of Judah and terminates in the crucified Christ himself as bait.

What for me is so fetching about this drawing is the excellent taper, or action, of the rod, which we might describe as medium-fast dry-fly. And note how the great God holds the rod more skillfully and sensitively than in any other ancient illustration I've seen. Especially note His left, or line, hand poised for work. He might well have shot a cast along with the best of us, had He guides on his rod for a long line.

I know, too, that back in the sixties, the experts at the Golden Gate Casting Club in San Francisco were thinking about the placement of the feet for the best distance casting. One theory put forward exactly describes this God's pedal position. Isn't it amazing how the entire stance is altogether contemporary?

And then look at that line and lure. How like an old Davis Pop Gear, those strings of "cowbells" that might extend a full yard or more for deep trolling. The terminal crucified Christ as lure is remarkably in proportion to the hook—and in scale with our own modern hardware. Even the hook itself is more carefully bent and barbed than in other such images, at least in my experience. No comment on the poor old devil of a Leviathan, except to say that it looks like nothing so much as a grotesque skulpin. This skulpin-Satan masks what might be part and parcel of that maternal energy of the waters from which we all emerged in the beginning, and which, according to psychoanalytic theory, we must combat in order to gain independent personhood.

I suspect that the anonymous creator of this work was an angler who knew fishing and its tackle, as well as religious iconography and theology. It's all too canny to be otherwise.

Angling and the Pastoral

A sign of the times is that ever increasing breed, the urban angler living far removed in fact and in spirit from the fishing of which he dreams. More and more, this city fisherman resorts to fantasy, conjuring the fishing that is so difficult to experience in actuality but for which there are ever proliferating virtual substitutes.

Youngish men and women, in the shanks of their lives, find themselves sadly short of the leisure time that fishing has traditionally presumed essential. They struggle to raise their families and cope with fourteen-hour workdays. With precious few moments to themselves, in some desperation, these new anglers sneak away to fly shops during lunch hours, steal moments for TV or video fishing, take a moment now and then to tie a fly, read a fishing book or magazine. Some find comfort in Trout Unlimited. And now the Internet. All of it a fantasy life that takes some of the pressure off the intense need to get out there on the stream and actually fish.

But there is really nothing new in this predicament. We may be certain that when men and women first organized themselves into cities some five thousand years ago, they soon felt a keen nostalgia for the country life, the rural life, they had left behind in order to experience the riches of the city. They must have felt alienated from nature. Admittedly, and like us, they likely romanticized and mythologized what they felt was the natural simplicity and tranquillity of the old life. And surely in their longing, like our own, they hoped that their ancient version of the weekend in the country would restore them.

That therapeutic weekend in the country, at the lake, on the stream, derives from one of the great organizing ideas in human culture: the myth of the pastoral world, perhaps the only major cultural fiction that has remained essentially unchanged over five thousand years of recorded human experience and imagination.

I am indebted here to the late John McDonald, historian of fly fishing and editor of *Fortune* magazine,[18] who in the introductory chapters to his *Quill Gordon*[19]) taught us to understand the central role of the pastoral ideal in angling.

It was the Greek poet Theocritus who in the third century B.C. gave literary form to the pastoral idea. His poems, or idylls, defined the genre and were extremely popular.

The pastoral presents a landscape of grassy meadows, hills, and dales, of lovely skies of deepest blue accented by the friendliest of clouds. It is a landscape of groves and shade, of pure springs and brooks (perfect for trout and mayfly), of singing birds and gently grazing sheep. All was innocence, repose, and harmony. Into this loveliness, enter its essential cast of characters—the shepherd and shepherdess—to tend their flocks or care for their bees, to pipe and sing their songs of love. Eternal youth and an effortless, cheerful, guileless life was their portion. If there was community in this landscape, it followed a primitive sort of communism, with neither strife nor want nor enmity.

For the Greeks it was that already long-lost golden age, which, in their imagination, was associated with the region of Arcadia on the Peloponnese, a golden age of which men and women have never ceased to dream. It is always a similar vision, with a simple tale to tell, of the pastoral world that lies deep in the imagination of all us, especially anglers.

We moderns have lost touch with the shepherd and shepherdess, but their situation still moves us. The pastoral idea is so pervasive and subtle that it even crops up in John Ford's 1939 film *Stagecoach* when John Wayne, as the Kid, tells his new love Dallas (Claire Trevor) that they should try to escape to his special place below the border, where there is safety amid trees, grass, and water. In a similar vein, there are those today who like to speak of the pre-European West as a sort of lost golden age of pastoral perfection.

After Theocritus, the great Roman poet Virgil composed his *Eclogues,* pastoral poems in which, McDonald points out, the first threatening clouds crossed the skies of the ideal. The city began to encroach upon the rural scene, and tensions rose.

But Western culture was thoroughly imbued now with the pastoral. Especially during the Renaissance, there were numbers of highly refined pastoral poems, dramas, and operas. In England, in 1496, that unknown author of the *Treatyse of Fysshynge Wyth an Angle* firmly placed fly fishing itself in the realm of the pastoral. And that Elizabethan man-of-all-work Sir Philip Sidney published his immensely popular pastoral *Arcadia.* Shakespeare, in turn, shows us the beauties of the pastoral life as well as its ironic limitations in *As You Like It.* And, should one want a short but striking discussion of the claim of the pastoral—the purely natural—versus denatured, scientifically manipulated nature, see the fourth act of Shakespeare's *A Winter's Tale.*[20] Next came Izaak Walton himself with his *Compleat Angler* of 1653, to fix sport fishing precisely and forever within the pastoral ideal. We know exactly where we are when, on his walk out of London to the River Lea, he encounters the milkmaid who sings for him Marlowe's famous "Come Live With Me and Be My Love."

But, of course, the ideal is deeply flawed. If in Virgil and later in Shakespeare we are brought to see the ironies and disappointments of it in literature, surely those first city folk of five thousand years ago must also have felt that their weekends in the country never quite measured up to their anticipation. All those wet Sundays, cold and miserable, when no fish rise. We wish we had stayed at home. The ideal, in fact, exists only rarely, and imperfectly. Still, even John Wayne's character feels the promise of that gentle life and is willing to risk everything on a run for it.

As McDonald says, rural people know better than to idealize the country. They know how tough country life can be—and usually is. In small, we anglers know very well how weather and water conditions can drive us in and make us regret going out in the first place. We all have known the hostility of nature and often suspect that she cares not a whit about us. But still we yearn for her pleasures and comforts. We never give up their pursuit.

McDonald goes on to state that the pastoral myth itself is an act of the strictly urban imagination—which is to say it's the stuff of city folks and their driven lives. He says, "When a city person walks in the country, it's a pastoral."[21] And his observations become his "pastoral memory." McDonald might just as well have said this of the angler who yearns for the pastoral experience and seeks to reinforce its values in himself whenever he can get to the stream—or its virtual substitute.

McDonald points out that the great eighteenth-century philosopher Jean-Jacques Rousseau may be credited with the first major break with the pastoral tradition when he introduced botany, and the botanist, into the equation. Our ancient Arcadian shepherd and shepherdess, those wise and gentle elders, were never keen observers of nature: they were not naturalists. They accepted their physical world without question, or even curiosity.

Then with the Enlightenment, with science and analysis, things changed. Enter modern skepticism. But even Rousseau couldn't free himself entirely from the romance of the pastoral. His modern botanist was beguiled back into the old ideal by the very experience of collecting and describing the nature he so carefully observed. In the same way, a modern angler struggles to find his way back into the tradition through, for instance, stream entomology and close attention to the environment.

That modern humans are seriously alienated from themselves, each other, their labor, and from nature is a commonplace of modern thought. Given this condition of alienation, we humans are forever straining to reunite ourselves with nature and all that is "natural." One has only to look at popular advertising to see how intense and perhaps futile this effort is. Ralph Waldo Emerson warned us against deliberately going out in search of nature and her benefactions. Nature, if we are truly ready for her, ought rather to come upon us, he said (with what John Keats called that "fine suddenness"), in a single blade of grass in our own back garden.

Perhaps most interesting is McDonald's explanation of the transformation of ancient sustenance-fishing, with all its dangers and melancholy, into fishing as sport and play, into fishing as a gentle and contemplative recreation. To transform so dour and tough an occupation into the cheerful, bucolic, gentle pursuit laid out in Walton and the author of the *Treatyse* is a cultural and socioeconomic coup of the first order.

McDonald explains that newly conceived sport fishing derived its tools from that old and severe occupational fishing, its idea of sport and its aesthetic from hunting, and its site of action, ethic, and spirit from the myth of the pastoral. This is the cultural transformation wrought by that unknown master of the *Treatyse* and by Walton. Conjoined, they have given us angling as we know it today.

Hunting, we are reminded, because of its violence, is excluded from the pastoral experience. Only riding to the hounds can approach the pastoral because of its reduced emphasis on the kill. How curious it is that killing fish has never in the human psyche been regarded quite as real killing. Hunting is a heroic sport, epic in its literary dimension, whereas fishing, especially trout fishing, partakes of the lyrical and serene, and so the pastoral. In that tradition we learn that there is much more to fishing than merely catching fish.

The author of the *Treatyse* advises that we should tune our-selves to the natural world around us. We should expect trout to be challenging to catch, and we should carefully limit our harvest of them.

If our attitude about killing fish is curious, it is more cu-rious still that the pastoral ideal introduced into angling in England between 1420 and 1653 was, after Walton, largely deserted. Mark Browning in his recent *Haunted by Waters*,[22] observes that after Walton the myriad English angling writers and authorities turned to the technology of fishing to enable the angler to catch as many and as big fish as possible. The English emphasis has remained there to this day. Interest-ingly enough, Browning finds, it is Americans, American writ-ers, and American authorities who, clinging to the ideals of Walton and program of the *Treatyse,* have taken up and pro-tected the values of the pastoral myth as central to fishing.

I've worried before in these essays about what I fear is often emotional posturing about the beauties of nature in overheated writing about fly fishing. Too often we may pro-fess to feel what we think we ought to feel. We have been programmed to believe that no matter what, we should love Nature with that capital letter. But this insistence only affirms the presence of that pastoral mythology deep inside us. The greater our sense of loss of contact with nature, the more intense will be our effort to affirm and regain it at any cost.

And when we cannot regain nature herself, we will turn to virtual, even cybernetic, substitutes. The danger is that we may be increasingly taken up by our fascination with the tech-nology of our sport rather than the spiritual enhancement of life that the old pastoral tradition promised. We have become frantic in our own special new way. With so few fishing days at our discretion, we want to pile up big numbers of twenty-inchers—almost like shares of stock on the market.

The best and most poignant example of an angler who beat the rap of modernism and succeeded in joining the tech-nology of angling to its pastoral ideal is Theodore Gordon, who early retired to the Catskill Mountains of New York to fish his flies as a way of life. He died there in his pastoral retreat in 1915, achieving mythic status himself.

The trouble is that into Gordon's ideal landscape, the serenity of his Neversink River and its handsomely rising trout, there intruded not only cold, wet days and miserable nights, but the monster tuberculosis that killed him with thoroughly modern efficiency.

In the end, our angling lives seem sadly broken over pastoral longing, economic necessity, and the ravages of Gordon's disease.

Life and Death in Trout Art

Not long ago, my wife and I found ourselves walking the streets of downtown Livingston, Montana, on a beautiful midsummer evening in keen anticipation of fishing the renowned DePuy Spring Creek the next morning. Never mind that as it turned out, gales of wind would blow us off the water. Knowing nothing as yet of those threatening winds, we were excited by the near saturation of appealing trout art in the local shops.

The pleasure and concentration of it got me to thinking about the origins of trout-fishing art. Fishing has always been the most intensely literary of sports, and angling is certainly distinguished among them for its contribution to world literature, Izaak Walton's *Compleat Angler* of 1653. But what can we say about other forms of trout art, which today seem so much in vogue?

Though not trained in art history or music theory, I'm bold enough to write here about two works of angling art from the nineteenth century: a piece of music and a painting—each titled "The Trout," and each about the death of its respective fish.

The piece of music is the brightest, happiest work of art imaginable. The painting, on the other hand, is almost terrifying in its violence and brutality.

About the music first. Franz Schubert was on a walking trip with his friend the singer Vogl in the mountains of Austria in July 1819. They visited the home of a friend, whose eight lovely daughters pleased the dashing young men immensely, causing them to linger. Their host, an amateur cellist, asked Schubert for a piano quintet that he and friends could play together at a musical evening. And so Schubert wrote his Quintet in A, op. 114, which came to be known as "The Trout" for its use of one of his songs. "The Trout" has become one of the most dearly loved of all chamber works. Its exhilarating music is irresistible.

This quintet features an unusual combination of instruments: a single violin, a viola, cello, piano, and double bass—exactly tailored to the local ensemble of music makers.

It is in the fourth movement of the work that Schubert employs his own song "Die Forelle" (1817) as theme, working several happy "trout" variations upon it. But the trout poem by C.F.D. Schubart on which "Die Forelle" is based is by our post-Romantic standards insipid and Disneylike in its sentimentality about animals and nature. Here are some bits of it patched together in translation:

> The brook so gaily rippling,
> There flashed a lively trout.
> But soon there came an angler,

> With rod and line and hook,
> To catch the fish that swam there,
> So happy in the brook.
> The trout snapped up his bait.
> He twitched his rod and caught him.
> And sad at heart and grieving,
> I saw the victim die.

Luckily, we do not hear those verses in the quintet, which leaves them unsung and forgotten. What remains is the music, reflecting the pleasures of the stream and the fish within it rather than the death of Schubart's pathetic trout.

Then there is French Realist Gustave Courbet's painting *The Trout*. It fills its frame—a big, heavy-bellied brown trout hauled up on the shore of lake or stream, dying a terrible death, line disappearing down its gullet, probably to a baited hook spilling blood from the great fish's gills. The colors are dark and ruthless, the form of the fish coarse. As we gaze at the picture, we are spared nothing. The trout's sentient eye, filled with fear, pain, and desolation, holds the angler in its supplication—or perhaps accusation.

Gustave Courbet's The Trout

Schubert's music warms us, refreshes us, and convinces us of the beauty and joy in all created things. It is uncritical, accepting, and healing. Courbet's painting, on the other hand, rubs our noses in the depravity of the world, the symbol of which is the painful death inflicted on this powerful animal.

In fact, this brute fish, its painter himself a known fisherman, has been regarded as a sort of self-portrait of the artist, a man whose aspect women had called animal, others oxlike. The dying trout may represent, as has been suggested, Courbet's suffering while imprisoned in Paris in the winter of 1871–1872. As a radical socialist, he was falsely arrested for the destruction of Napoleon's triumphal column after the fall of the Commune of Paris. If the painting is allegorical, the theme is a favorite with the realists of Courbet's group—that of a being pursued unto death.

Disparate visions of the world and our place in it dominate these two early examples of trout-fishing art. The death of the trout, as narrated in Schubert's song, counts for little with us. There is nothing real about that fish, whose suffering is only the posturing of a lesser romantic poet. What counts for Schubert, what pours forth from his unforgettable music and recalls and restores our experience of youth, love, beauty, and nature, is, paradoxically, the trout's life.

The suffering and death of Courbet's trout is, on the other hand, utterly realistic, and we are subsumed in it. Here, life is little more than being pursued unto death—awful, meaningless, cruel, and forgotten even before it is noticed. The painting suggests that dying is what animals like us properly do.

These works of art suggest a polarity, a line of tension between life and death, along which we arrange, or try to arrange, our lives. Indeed, as has often been said, the trout is the canary down in the dark and poisonous mines of our lives—where, of course, there is always the chance that the bird will live to sing.

Some of It in Verse

Our Opening Days
For Elaine and Lisa
and Their Dad

Our parents,
Never taking education lightly,
Always guaranteed
That on opening day of trout season,
They'd write excuses
For us to have a truant day.

Al and I,
With boxes of flies and cans of worms,
Somehow got up Boulder Creek
In the raw and predawn hours,
To race at setting up,
Each to outdo the other.

"Come to attention and salute the flag
Before you dare to cast," Al demanded—
A sort of ritual in our faintly hostile haste.

The cold was always awful.
The water high and roily,
Brown and mica-flecked,
Pouring down the canyon in a torrent,
Obscuring every hole and riffle,
Making the creek alien, violent, dangerous.

Our boxed arrays of flies were useless.
Worms on size 10 Eagle Claws
With three split-shot
Alone made any sense.

We almost always
Got a strike—right away.
Or likelier still, a snag.
But maybe a trout—

Maybe two, I don't remember very well.
But not many and most likely small.
Miserably cold and frustrated,
We were ready to quit for home by nine.

Down the canyon
To stop in town at the bakery for the donuts,
Fresh and hot, that Dad let us eat straight from the machine
With a can of that vile bakery coffee: a restorative—
A sign that all might still be well . . .

I think we usually ended up back in school at noon,
Tired and distracted by images
Etched of the torrential creek
Residual still behind our eyes,
The heft of the rod still in our hands,
Sensing the drift of our worms,
Hunting trout so hard to find . . .

But the donuts
Right from the machine, the bakery warmth,
Even the coffee,
Our parents' good faith in our fishing,
That exhausted numbness of the afternoon,
Tied us together in secret ways
That helped to teach us how to love.

For Uncle Art
September 12, 1988

They worked hard that afternoon at the Boulder City
Bakery in order to get through early enough
To fish awhile in the beaver ponds out east of
Town, a quarter mile or so up the

Creek from where it crossed old Valmont
Road, "way out in the country," back then, when
Beaver still dammed and made black
Pools that trout found out and Uncle Arthur, too,
Who understood such water and would
Take us kids out there that day
With Mervin Eggleston, I think . . . so self-absorbed
Was I in what it meant to me to
Be going after those wild trout with
My new fly rod and automatic reel—the best of
Christmas presents yet and still.

Somehow, in the beavers' chain of lodges I
Found a pond, small, deep, mysterious,
Opaque and rich in the loam-reflecting blackness.
How could I have known that trout might
Be right there? For there they were! And
To my stunned surprise I hooked
And lost one right away, only to be left bewildered,
Breathless, in the grip of the thing,
Fumbling now with another worm,
Sending it down to try again.
And again there was that tap and tug, the bite . . .
Somehow the hook got set, and up that seven-incher
Came from the depths, numinous in silver, red,
And green, from the black and crystal
Water to my feet: this first wild
Trout in my young life, just for me,
All things else surpassing.

Today, I learned that Uncle Art will fish no more . . .
Anyhow, the beaver and the trout are gone,
The countryside a mess,
The creek now drainage for the sorry city.
And I've grown old, trailing Uncle Art a bit,
But committed now to fish for him
Wherever I can find that black and
Crystal water of my heart.

A Ghost for Boulder Creek

Percy Oliver Wickstrom

> William Bolcom sat at the piano—
> A concert of a winter afternoon—
> To play a rag called "Graceful Ghost,"
> That he had written for his father
> When he died.
> I listened—with regret
> That I had written nothing
> For my father when he died in '81.
> And so today . . .

Dad took me up the creek
Those Sunday mornings, early,
When the canyon seemed deserted,
And I could fish a favorite stretch
Behind El Vado Lodge.
My father waited patiently while I
fished the pockets with hard black ants.

Fishing held no real interest for my dad.
His interest was in me—
To help and understand.
But he loved the two or three nice
Trout I often caught.
And there was nothing quite so fine
As that coffee and sweet-roll
Over the little fire he built,
My Dad,
Who understood such things.
Oh, Dear Graceful Ghost!

Worms for the Twenty-fifth of May[23]

A time for worms, this spring,
This morning, dark and cold as hell.
The water bronze and thick with mica flecks
To catch the dawn of Opening Day.
The angler's spirits go down with his worms
To make him wonder why he keeps on coming out
This early in the spring,
When only worms produce,
And then not very well . . .

Until—and suddenly—
He feels, from deep within a swirling eddy,
Up the line, through the rod, and to his hand
The trout's repeated tugs,
Tapping, snapping, at the invisible worm,
A signal to empty his head
Of all the conscious world
Except to time it right, to hook this fish!
Drive the steel home
Deep into its gullet bleeding.
To keep it!
Dead for a worm;
Dead for a springtime raw and cold—
A trout for the creel,
The privilege of its beauty
Now ritual of the table.

More likely, though, he sets the hook
Too soon, too late, too hard, too light,
(There're many ways to miss a fish).
And nothing's there, no trout, nothing,
Except perhaps a snag to break him off—
And make him wonder why he keeps on coming out

This early in the unforgiving spring
When only worms produce . . .
And then not very well.

Back Then in Boulder

We used to think an angler smoked a pipe
And kept snelled flies around his hat,
A beat-up, poor old felt that stunk.
A leather-bound and willow creel
Held both his trout and fly book,
Made by "Commonsense."
Clumsy boots and ragged coat
Completed this original, whose style
The stream itself had wrought.

This angler never knew the
Regulating catalogs that systemize
The angler of today, replete
With carbon rod, designer vest, and
Slung with technologies the like of which
This old-timer could not have dreamed
Back then, when automatic reels whirred in
Level lines of amber silk, size D or E,
Up to level leaders, three feet of gut—
Dropper and point—for a Gray Hackle Yellow
and Rio Grande King.

The Red and the Black
(With a nod to Stendhal)

This buffalo plaid upon my arm
Has the red of flies I sometimes cast.
No living fly with such a red as that, I think . . .
But the black
Is the black of ants and beetles
And the myriad chironomids
That stuff the guts of trout—
The black that makes trout fall
For my black flies and thoughts.

But I'd rather think of Royal Coachmen—
That blood-red body part
Working its spell in God knows
What mysterious way
To raise a trout,
Make me love my shirt,
And turn my thoughts from black to red.

The Kells Blackwater: May 1976

Natural and supernatural with the self-same ring are
wed. As man, as beast, as ephemeral fly begets,
Godhead begets Godhead, for things below are copies,
the Great Smaragdine tablet said.

— W. B. Yeats, "Supernatural Songs" 99,
"Ribh Denounces Patrick"

On the River now,
Fretful and on edge,
We wait to cast
To turbulent trout
Feeding in air and water
on the luxury of May.

But there are no trout, no flies.
The water's blank,
Shining, silver, perfect
For the birth of all that loveliness.
We yearn for the flies,
For heavy fish and pulsing rods.
We stare at the empty water
As though to force the hatch.

Until,
In his own perfected time
And near to our despair
A dun appears,
Herald to the myriad of his kind.
The Mayfly!
Ephemera danica coming down!
What shall we put up,[24]
nymph or dun or spinner?[25]
Riding the current of the moment
Motionless in natal amazement
Until, as to some signal of his life,
He lifts into that Irish sky—
Just enough blue to make yourself a shirt.[26]

Fish and bird are driven mad
For the richness of this provender.
But now, if things are right,
If Nature and our symbols coalesce,
Dun will change to spinner,
And—reaching Dectine's lips—
May cross the tongue of love
And in the ecstacy of her throat,
In that particular womb, get Cuchulain![27]

On this river-bar the flies appear and disappear,
My imitation lost among them.
Could this have been the Ford of the Woman Slaughter
Where he killed "thrice fifty queens?"[28]
("Cuchulain's life is woman's work.")[29]
Faithless and loyal, amorous and violent,
His ephemeral father forgotten in his boast of Lugh.[30]
Never aware of the insect's beauty, its formal achievement,
Its Virtue!
Its inseminate power forgotten for a mess of
Dog flesh,[31] ravens, his bowels in his hands,[32]
Ferdia dead,[33] Conla murdered on the strand,[34]
Oh Emer, Emer, Betrayed again![35]
He should have cast aside his Gae Bolga sex
And sought his father in his river in his month of May—
Like us: a rod of cane instead,
And put up nymph or dun or spinner.
No more his Hero's disappointment and love's despair.
(An angler's disappointment is enough,
however sound his wrist or true his cast.)

Ned[36] and I stare the River blind,
Flowing from the West of Kells
And beyond where Shannon moves slack
Between the Irish North and South.[37]
The cows are bull-less in the wet-green meadows
Of the everlasting valley,
Close to Tara and the long gaze dreaming into Ulster.
But I keep one eye set for fly and rising trout
And only then the other free and out of time
To search the West for Connacht's white-horned Bull
And Ulster's fabled Brown up North.[38]

Once, when life was big beyond any understanding,
Those bulls fought for days over all these hills.
Now again, this afternoon,
That Ulster prize might tear apart his Irish Kin
And, like Cuchulain, beyond any understanding,
Die in his turn, with a host of such good men
As Ned and I.

As angler (and as stranger) in this land,
I work these fish as I work these *words*
With stealth and not without misgiving,
On the lookout now for bulls as well:
Emblems of my fear—and all that I must lose.
Now all there is to do is watch and fish and hope—
Hope for maybe two good trout, and, Oh, my heart!
Exalted in the Mayfly,
Hope for the likes of Dectine and her mouth!

Once, long ago, she took a Mayfly in that mouth
And got a dark and disappointed Hero.
Now, we anglers settle for a great lot less in life.

But, once we've fished to this *Ephemera*
On his way to wondrous new paternity,
Once we've glimpsed the Bride,
Anxious in doubt, certain in Lust,
We fish the secret currents of the Self,
Luring back our wasted passion
In the dream of a Hero's birth and death,
Catching where we may furtive brief moments
Of darkest, sweetest love.

Indulgence on the Wharfe [39]

"Go ahead," he said,
"Make a fool of yourself,"
Said my host and ghillie,
An expert himself with the fly
On the Wharfe,
In the Dales.

He stretched full length
On the sloping lawn
Waiting for me to fish
The reach of water
He had pointed out.

In an agony of nerves,
I wished that I had never come,
When he said,
"Go ahead, make a fool of yourself."

That said,
I felt released.
He forgave in advance
My bumbling on his river.
All the misery eased off.
And with immense relief,
In something like a state of grace,
I waded in to do my work.

Quite at once the big brown took.

Song of The Letort Spring Run
Variation on a Theme by Ernest Schwiebert[40]
Music by John Patrick Thomas

Season's done: the Regulars gone home.
Night stirs.
Moon and mist float the deserted river.

The meadow ghosts arise.
Spectral lines whisper through the mists,
Falling touchless on the moon-drenched water.

Forgotten limestone anglers
With ring-and-keeper rods of greenheart
Work the black and silver stream.

Night-spun mayfiles dance their flickering death,
Marinaro out among them.
As Letort trout rise up to scorn his fame.

SONG OF THE LETORT SPRING RUN

Gordon Wickstrom

John Patrick Thomas
2000

1

mists,_____ Fall-ing touch-less on the moon - drenched wa - ter.

For - got - ten lime - stone an - glers With ring-and-keep-er rods of green - hart

Work the black and sil - ver stream. Night - spun may - flies Dance

2

their flick - 'ring death. Ma - ri - na - ro out a - mong them.

As Le - tort trout rise up to scorn his fame.

Hamburg 22.3.2000

In a New Jersey Garden

Some say the Hendrickson comes off
When the forsythia's in bloom.
But I say
Forsythia figures rods of cane
Bending under golden loads
On languidly recurving boughs
To make their airy casts.

Holy Saturday, 2001

Simile

A fish on the fly—
As alive in the hand
As a kite in the sky.

Amos 4:2

In his Compleat Angler, Izaak Walton remarks that "angling is much more ancient than the Incarnation of our Saviour; for in the prophet Amos mention is made of fish-hooks."

The Lord God hath sworn by his holiness that lo,
the days shall come upon you, that he will take you away
with hooks, and your posterity with fish-hooks.

The text is precise:
He will take us with his fishhooks,
This Fisher of Men.

Watching carefully
From deep within the waters of my life,
I have considered his baits—
And avoided them.

His oath will get no strike from me,
His hook barbed deep within my death.
I'll not be eaten by his thousands,
And least of all a symbol
Scratched in stone to call his name.

This Angler is insatiable.
Protesting his holiness,
His creel already full,
He stalks my days to come.
And in another season
Will angle for my posterity.

My position is that he
Leave my posterity alone
To swim the currents of their days
Wherever they should flow.

But should he hone his hooks against us,
And cast so nicely to us,
I guarantee that I will have
Such Revenges
I will lie on the bottom and sulk.

Betty Replies

Oh my dear,
Lest you fall to idolatry,
Remember the fish, mysterious, wily
And beauteous though it be,
Is only one of His miraculous creatures
Including you and me.

Best to hope that the Fisher of Men
Will catch us all—fathers, mothers, progeny—
Sulky and evasive though we be,
And spread us out on dewy grass, a delight to see,
Before gathering us into His capacious creel
To take us home.

—B.J.W.

A Golden Age

Back then,
Throughout the season,
Ferrules loosened,
Glue joints opened,
Tips snapped,
Reels jammed,
Lines and leaders rotted.
Snells broke,
Hooks as always snagged,
Hip boots leaked,
And ancient creels stank.

Back then,
And after all of that,
We had the winter off.
Pheasant, duck, and deer
Took up the autumn
While we forgot the trout.
Until one day,
In winter,
Around the solstice,
We awoke,
Unhinged, restless, craving,
Something missing.
A timely utterance gave relief.
To Fish!
It's nearly time again!

Dreaming of spring
Through stacks of catalogs,
Piles of tackle,
Restored and new:
Oiled-up reels, rewrapped guides,

Fresh gut ready for the glycerin mix,
That fragrant, stinking creel.
Planning new rods and reels,
A better line,
New flies of "yellow, and black, and pale,
and hectic red,"
Of memorial name and history
In a fly book holding more, more neatly.

Then, almost suddenly,
After winter's wait,
We were out there,
On the stream again
(Oh, the fragrance of that creel!),
Rushing like the water
Toward the trout we hoped to move.

A rough and ready Golden Age.
It might have lasted even until now . . .
Had not
Those marketeers got hold of us
And washed our ancient creels clean.

Aubade

O, Silken Loop of Line,
Unrolling in the Morning Light,
Sing! Sing of
Tracing and Retracing,
Turning and Returning,
Hov'ring, Searching,
Tight'ning, Loos'ning,
Winding, Finding,
Falling and Alighting,

Delighting
Every Hidden
Pool and Pocket,
Flat and Eddy,
Riffle, Run, and Rip,
Every Slick and Seam and Slot,
Of Purling River's Body.

O, Lovely Loop of Line,
Describing Every Curve,
Sing of Morning's Pleasure
And the Rise of My Trout's Love!

The Old-Timer

When I was five or six years old,
I walked downtown one day—
alone.

And past the Pine Street porch of the Tanner house
Where old Frank Tanner sat—gently
swinging.

"Hello, there, Old-timer," Frank called out,
His salutation in rhythm with his
swing.

I remember the feeling:
Suddenly a Somebody—
recognized!

Now, these long years later,
I walk that same way past that vacant
porch.

Longing still to be a Somebody:
An Old-timer—
recognized!

Three Masters of It

The Presence of Theodore Gordon

His sylvan life is our lost world.
—John McDonald, *Quill Gordon*

It is a bitter cold winter's night and I am far
away from the cheerful lights of town or city.
The north wind is shrieking and tearing at
this lonely house, like some evil demon wishful
to carry it away bodily or shatter it completely. The icy breath of this demon pen-
etrates through every chink and crevice, and
the wood-burning stove is my only companion. It is on nights such as these, after the
turn of the year, that . . . we return in spirit
to the time of trout rising in the pools. We
remember many days of glorious sport, and
then somehow our thoughts take a turn and
leap forward. Spring is near, quite near, and
it will soon be time to go fishing.
—*Theodore Gordon on the Neversink,
in John McDonald, Quill Gordon*

In the falling darkness of a winter afternoon, I sat
reading the notes and letters of America's foremost fly fisherman, Theodore Gordon. His personality, his voice, his spirit—whatever one calls
it—gained on me by the page, by the minute,
until, in a wonderful way, my reading conjured
what seemed Gordon's very presence. The experience was so compelling that it brought me
to my feet, book in hand, amazed, feeling

touched by that elegant, fragile, reclusive genius of the trout fly.

What I'd known of Gordon before, seemed, in this instant of his presence, fragmentary and unfocused. I knew that I must try to understand better this extraordinary man who more than any other gave a distinctly American cast to fishing the fly and suggested new and native ways of thinking and feeling about the experience.

Living his "sylvan life" in his beloved Catskill Mountains, he devoted nearly his entire adult life to fishing the fly for trout. He was to become a mythic figure, a man whose life is for us a glimpse back into what seems a little golden age. In our myth-dreaming, he models the ideal American angler's life.

Gordon was born to fortunate circumstances in Pittsburgh, Pennsylvania, on September 18, 1854. A small and delicate child who lost his father almost at once, he nevertheless became enthralled with fishing, especially during summers spent on the Pennsylvania limestone streams around Carlisle, holidays provided by his father's legacy.

The details of Gordon's biography are obscure and largely memorial; little of it is documentary. Several of his contemporaries knew a bit about him, dined out on it, and passed it on, but apparently none knew Gordon's whole story. He kept his counsel.

In any case, after spending the first half of his life in finance in the Northeast and in Savannah, where he had family connections and origins, his finances and health broke. In early retreat from active life, he seems to have lived for a time in comfort in West Haverstraw, New York, at the home of a relative, Theodore Gordon Peck, Sr. From here he made regular angling forays into the Catskills and Poconos. Sometime before 1905, he left the Peck home in favor of residence on the Neversink River in the Catskills, perhaps in the hope of benefiting from the mountain air. Whatever his motivation, the move brought him to a fine trout stream, where he lived almost as a recluse in a succession of uncomfortable farmhouses along the river.

Gordon's mother, Fanny Jones Gordon, chronically ill herself and anxious about her son's well-being alone up there in the mountains, paid Gordon regular summer visits. Tensions rose as they bore the burden of each other's illness. On occasion, Gordon complained to friends that his mother's condition was all too confining for him. But they got on, against the odds, both to die in 1915.

Gordon fished hard throughout each season, and read everything about fly fishing he could get his hands on, especially the English authors. From his reading he taught himself to tie the flies that would make him famous. Season by season, he became more and more the master angler/fly tier of the Neversink—the complete American fly fisher.

Following the collapse of the family railroad interests, Gordon's paternal legacy was seriously diminished, but he was able to augment his meager income by dressing flies to order at $1.25 the dozen for a clientele of prosperous, vacationing metropolitan anglers who came to the Catskills as to Mecca, seeking to lionize Gordon and fish his definitive dressings.

Gordon was an inveterate correspondent with family, friends, and other anglers. A letter of inquiry to England's great Frederick Halford, the father of the dry fly, elicited from Halford on February 22, 1890, a full set of his new and revolutionary dry flies. That was a seminal moment for American anglers, for thus the dry fly arrived in America to be naturalized to these shores by Theodore Gordon. Though Gordon was neither the only nor the first to take up the floating fly in America, his study, practice, and ensuing reputation were to do for the dry what Hamlet says the actor does for his time: show its "form and pressure."

Though Gordon took to Halford's dry flies with enthusiasm, he realized that they would not readily suit the requirements of our often rougher American rivers and streams, with their more diverse hatches of insects. Halford's flies would

Theodore Gordon rests with a friend on the Neversink.

require considerable adaptation, and the addition of wholly
new patterns of imitation.

In 1890, there was no full and systematic entomology of
American stream insects, and Gordon fondly hoped that some
American would soon rise to the occasion. His own efforts to
classify the mayfly were only tentative. Still, he was always
learning. "We can never learn all there is in fly fishing," he
wrote on May 14, 1912, "but we can keep an open mind, and
not be too sure of anything. . . . It is a fascinating business."[41]
Constant learning was what he said he liked best about fishing,
its never-ending challenge and novelty. He was as without
dogma as any mortal could be.

Though companions in the culture of angling, Gordon
and Halford were profoundly different. The English Halford,
ever the dogmatist, insisted that as a matter of angling deco-
rum, scientific rectitude, and social status, fishing the dry fly,
and fishing it properly, on his chalk streams, was the solely
acceptable behavior. Not so for our Gordon, whose mind

was of that restless, inquiring, and pragmatic American bent, always experimental and always open to the next idea.

Gordon's work at his vise initiated perhaps the most significant movement in American fly tying: the Catskill School. On the assumption that a fly ought to suggest, if not imitate, insects actually encountered on our American streams, Gordon gave his dressings a sparse, somber-bright delicacy achieved by slender, nicely tapered, rather short dubbed or quill bodies. Hackles were selected for their stiff, glossy barbs in exactly the right duns, creams, gingers, and browns. The favored wing material, and basic to the genius of the Catskill School, was the lemon barred side of the wood duck. These delicately barred feathers suggested better than any other the even more delicately marked venation of a mayfly's wing. The tail, though in some cases also of wood duck, more frequently employed stiff, slightly elongated hackle barbs. These helped the flies to "cock," to sit up high and dry on the surface, as Halford insisted they must. Finally, the heads of Catskill drys are idiomatic, wonderfully slender and neat, and at the height of the style preserve a bit of bare steel between the head and the eye of the hook. These flies speak of Nature itself and astonish with their superb, withal conservative beauty.

A representative half dozen patterns developed by the Catskill tiers would include the Light Cahill, the Hendrickson, the March Brown, the Grey Fox, and the Quill Gordon, along with that great searching fly, the Fan Wing Royal Coachman. The Quill Gordon was Theodore Gordon's emblematic contribution to what we might call "the American Collection." It remains essential to any well-appointed fly box.

In his earlier years, Gordon remarked time and again on how difficult it was for him to get fly-tying materials, there being for practical purposes no American suppliers. Ordering from England, the only other alternative, was not without its frustrations. He wanted stiffer, glossier, more web-free hackles than the English were content to use. He was a stickler for getting just the right shades of color and textures into his flies. Forever on the lookout for them in milliners' shops, among costumers and fellow fly tiers, and on the birds he shot—wherever silk, feather, and fur might be found—he bummed, borrowed, and begged whatever he could. And returned in kind.

Far from becoming a Halfordian purist, Gordon never gave up entirely his straps of two or three wet flies fished up or down the stream as conditions required. He was an acknowledged master of that technique. Nor did he shun the bucktail come a new spring with its high, rough waters. He loved everything about fishing and fish and wrote enthusiastic letters about the latest Hildebrandt spoons for pike, about casting for bass, and about his yearning to catch a muskie. He was indeed the complete angler.

Unhappily, there were days when he could cast no flies, nor anything else, days when he was too ill to stray far from his bed. He spoke of a perishing "goneness"—"I will be working cheerfully at something" he wrote on February 12, 1915, "and this goneness will suddenly grab me."[42] On these days he contented himself with tying flies, reading and writing, or perhaps just dreaming of the river, on which, he could admit, he was not as strong a wader as he would like to be, his "thin legs" sometimes letting him down.

Some winter days, too impossibly cold in his drafty old farmhouse to sit at his table by the kitchen window to tie flies, he might be compelled just to hover over his woodstove, feeding it constantly. On one of those days, he discovered that he could sit by it and, without his vise, hand-hold the hooks, on which he could tie quite nicely, especially the hackle patterns.

The 1880s were a watershed of development for fly fishing in America and England. For Gordon the high point must have been the arrival of Halford's dry flies at the very end of the decade, but he had always taken a lively interest in the development of new tackle and techniques.

He welcomed, for instance, flies tied on eyed hooks as Halford advocated. Their advantage over gut snells or loops wrapped onto blind hook shanks was clearly apparent to him.

He was enthusiastic about the new split-cane rods. Their fast, stiff, six-sided superiority, especially in the tapers of Hiram Leonard, were to carry the day for fly fishing. A Leonard tournament model of ten feet and six ounces was Gordon's favorite, but how a man of his slight build could wield a rod of that magnitude all day, we well might wonder.

Essential for the new rods were oil-impregnated tapered silk lines. Fly lines now had sufficient weight for long casts and could be greased to float. When cast from the new rods, these lines made possible dry-fly fishing as we know it—false casting to dry the fly, driving it well upstream into the wind, and then controlling its drift. It had to have been exciting.

On the darker side, Gordon witnessed the virtual disappearance of the beloved eastern brook trout from its native range in the eastern states. Floods, droughts, industrial pollution, lumbering, and overfishing: all contributed to the lovely but vulnerable "trout's" near demise (Gordon always resisted thinking of the brook trout as a char; for him the brookie was a trout, and that was that). Rescue of the fisheries came with the introduction of the German brown trout in 1883. Gordon welcomed the foreigner. It was exactly the right breed at the right moment to close the circuit of success for the dry-fly's development. The "yellow trout's" readiness to feed at the surface, its ability to thrive in warmer, sometimes moderately polluted water, its fecundity, and its size recommended it, even if it was not as succulent at table as the brook.

Later, when from California the rainbow began to appear in eastern waters, he was expansive in his approval of what he felt were the excelling qualities of that western trout now come east.

Today we may flinch at Gordon's frequent remarking on the many and heavy "baskets" of trout he killed. He writes, "On one opening day I made a basket of thirty-eight good fish during a snowstorm."[43] We read on, somehow expecting him to regret his kill. But he does not. A quarter of a century into our practice of catch-and-release, we wonder how it could ever have been thus.

He deeply regretted the increasing privatization of the most productive stretches on the Catskill streams by the rich and powerful. The wealth of big-city club men was too much for many farmers along the streams to resist, and so they sold their leases. When these vacationing anglers sought out Gordon to claim him for their own, he would turn down their invitations to fish their well-stocked and private waters. The Dean of the Catskills said that he preferred to work over the fewer and tougher trout in free public water.

Gordon was on every bit as intimate and eloquent terms with the natural world as was Izaak Walton two hundred years earlier. In fact, there are those who have called Gordon the American Walton. His notes and letters are punctuated with keen and appealing observations on the rivers, forests, and fields around him. Not to fishing alone, he was devoted to his shotgun and upland shooting and was afield whenever his wintertime health and the open season permitted. He responded to nature in one breath as a problem in conservation and in the next as an aesthetic pleasure.

He thought fly fishing an ideal activity for women and wondered that more had not taken it up. We know of but one woman, other than his mother, who played a role in his life, a mysterious young woman of whom he wrote, on October 20, 1906, "The best chum I ever had in fishing was a girl, and she tramped just as hard and fished quite as patiently as any man I ever knew."[44] Among the few photographs of Gordon, perhaps the most fetching shows this unknown lady, wading in her skirts, with fly rod well bent into a fish. Gordon wades at her side in an attitude suggesting admiration. Who was she? What became of her? We want her story—a story it seems we are not to have.

Our Gordon indulged in none of the cant and self-promotion of today's aggressive fly-fishing professionals who so dominate the sport. He would have rejected out of hand even the suggestion that he was what we regard today as an "expert." Modesty defined the man.

Out of his intense experience with trout and fly, he contributed what, in that modesty, he called his "notes" to England's influential *Fishing Gazette,* which accorded him great respect and renown as the premier American angler. After 1900, his notes also appeared in the American magazine *Forest and Stream,* but during his lifetime, he would remain better known in England than in his homeland. Writing without any hint of self-consciousness, and seemingly without plan, he appears merely to have wanted to talk with other anglers, to compare his notes with theirs in his effort to continue learning.

Gordon's failure to collect, for whatever reason, his material into a book—though he may have been doing so at his death—doubtless kept him from publishing his definitive experience of fly fishing to a larger American angling public, and so he was to remain imperfectly known until 1947, when, with the publication of his letters and notes,[45] he at last took his pride of place in the fellowship of anglers.

Theodore Gordon, "the Sage of the Neversink," died at sixty-one on the first of May, 1915, in Bradley, New York, close by the Neversink. Tuberculosis, which may have been stalking him all his life, almost certainly was the killer. He lies in a family vault beside his mother in tiny Marble Cemetery in the East Village of Manhattan. His reach of the Neversink lies buried deep under a reservoir of the same name.

Theodore Gordon defined a fully human life in the cast of a fly to a trout, and through his account of it, became a living presence to me on that special winter afternoon.

Vince Marinaro: On the Point of Balance

The Two Faces of Janus

Time moves slowly in fly fishing. The last time it moved appreciably in the United States was with Theodore Gordon.
— John McDonald

It moved again in 1950.

Various of his followers in Pennsylvania's Cumberland Valley called him "Papa." Vince Marinaro, that brilliant, passionate, and irascible master of the fly, in 1950, on the point of balance between past and future of the twentieth century, published his *A Modern Dry-fly Code*,[46] giving America its first thoroughly original work on fly fishing. It changed our sport forever.

We attribute to Marinaro the development and codification of what we know about fishing the tiniest flies and flies imitating land-born terrestrial insects that happen into the water. We think of the famous jassid, with its jungle cock nail[47] suggesting the insect's opaque body; of Marinaro's powerful innovation in the configuration of the dry fly—his "thorax" tie, with its high, clear-sailing mayfly wing amidships, X-tied with splayed hackle around a prominent thorax. At least as important is the way he opened our eyes to, and taught us to fish, that previously "unseen" wonderful hatch, the tiny *Tricorythodes,* without which today our fly fishing would hardly be imaginable.[48] And more.

Marinaro was indeed the "papa" of a revelation, if not a revolution, and, I believe, the first fully modern angler. He stood in the tall grasses along his beloved Letort like Janus, that Roman deity with two faces, one looking back with deep admiration, even longing, toward the origins and traditions of fly fishing in the British Isles and early North America, the other gazing out at new horizons in analysis, technology, and science in the second half of the twentieth century. To his east was the immense achievement of the nineteenth century, its history, romance, and tradition; to his west the challenge of innovation and fresh, imaginative solutions to the age-old problems of the fly fisher.

To understand Marinaro, we need to listen carefully to the *Code,* to the dual messages of this Janus. When Marinaro writes of the past, of Halford and Skues and Harding, of Gordon and the early Americans, he uses language and imagery reminiscent of their time and place, language richer in metaphor, more expansive and classical in its resources—more Romantic, one might say. As though to honor the past, he tunes himself to what he so admires in Halford's style, as if hoping to acquire some of its luster. He seeks communion with the giants of angling history whom he so greatly admired. But, let him shift in a single paragraph, turning 180 degrees, to thoughts about the present and the future, and his style quickly takes on a different tone, dryer, more economic, analytic, and scientific. He knows and understands where he has been and where he wants to go. The reader feels and hears the emotion of ideas in his writing, this Janus standing pivotal in the twentieth century.

We may be tempted to speculate about where such pivotal figures come from. Do people of genius somehow choose just the right time and place in which to appear? Or is it that time and place choose them? Was Marinaro somehow chosen when first he came to Cumberland County and Dickinson Law School in 1934, with the Letort itself flowing through town, as yet unappreciated in modern angling

Vincent Marinaro along Penns Creek.

practice, not yet a part of our literature and collective experience?

A subtle movement was already under way to shift the focus of American fly fishing from New York's fabled Catskills to this rural Pennsylvania county, and the Cumberland Valley streams that Gordon himself had often fished with his wet flies as a boy and young man. Edward Hewitt and George La Branche had begun to visit these waters, trailing the glories of the New York tradition behind them. The Pennsylvania limestone streams were new and exciting, profoundly different from Gordon's Neversink. All was ripe for discovery—ripe for the likes of a Marinaro.

A new breed of local, serious angler had already begun to appear. In the 1940s these capable, resourceful, innovative men formed the Fly Fishers' Club of Harrisburg and challenged each other to develop ideas and tactics for their highly specialized limestone waters and their difficult trout.

Vince Marinaro and his good friend and equally noted

habitué of the Letort Charlie Fox brought to the club their fast-growing experience in fish culture, entomology, and fishing the Letort's maddeningly difficult currents and insects.

I want to emphasize that Marinaro and his ideas did not develop in an intellectual angling vacuum, but within the matrix of this extraordinary bunch of Harrisburg fly fishers. They had to have been an inspiration, being, as they were, highly competitive, bursting with fly-fishing ideas and experience. Genius thrives in just such a milieu, and Marinaro was no exception. One has only to think, for instance, of the young Shakespeare's coming down to London to a new, fully professional theatre marvelously suited to his immense talent.

Of special interest is the practice of the Harrisburg Fly Fishers at their luncheon meetings to read short, formal papers about their ideas and discoveries. Marinaro, though, appears to have listened more than he wrote.[49] These anglers must have sensed that they occupied a special time and place and wanted carefully to record their work. That work, and Marinaro's own great insights, came to fruition in 1950 with the publication of *A Modern Dry-fly Code,* a summa of all that Marinaro had experienced and thought in the 1940s.

The personal and professional development that brought him fame in the 1950s was purchased through early discipline and determined effort. It could not have been easy, coming down out of the mountains of western Pennsylvania, with its freestone creeks, to the gentler Cumberland Valley. He came as a first-generation son of a tightly-knit, extended Italian family—his father but one of the seven members who immigrated to this country. Vincent brought with him that all-too-typical burden of having to prove himself in the highly competitive New World. The implications of this common psychological baggage are well known. Young Vincent was only six when his father, Giuseppe, a successful entrepreneur, merchant, and pasta maker, died. His mother Rosina, with the help of the boy's uncle Vincent, a priest in Butler, Pennsylvania, had all the care of her children, including that special fishing son whose imagination must have been all for the future his father hoped for him.

His brother Nicholas has said of Vincent that he loved nature, loved to stuff his pockets with olives and cheese and take off into the woods alone to prowl and to fish. By age ten he was accomplished on the violin, but his mother had to admonish him for hiding copies of *Outdoor Life,* with Ray Bergman's influential columns, under his music in the piano bench.

For Vincent, and numberless young people like him, the main road to achievement and advancement in America was through the professions, which required a solid education. Fortunately, his late father had been able to provide for one. Educated at the Dickinson Law School in Carlisle, Pennsylvania, Marinaro subsequently made corporate tax law his bread and butter with the Commonwealth of Pennsylvania at Harrisburg. There he had a lifelong and noteworthy career without ever formally coming to the bar.

Cutting a distinctive image with his chiseled Roman features, his piercing eyes, insistent speech, and Dutch Master cigars, he must have been the very model of a smart, charismatic, aggressive young Italian American on the way up in a wide-open America—all the while clinging fiercely to his Italian heritage and traditions.

His accomplishments were wide-ranging. The violin, shotgunnery, gunstock design, archery, photography, entomology, replication of Native American crafts, the lecture platform, and even a claim on the culinary arts—all vied for attention with his mastery of fishing, its tackle, and traditions. Probing scholarship and an experimentally inclined curiosity made him, perhaps, the first intellectual of American fly-fishing history.

Physically as well as intellectually gifted, he was said to have had phenomenal eyesight and the keenest powers of observation. His bent of mind was for the theoretical. His broad, contextual thinking brought everything imaginable to bear on an idea—its literature, its science, its lore, its romance—anything that might expand and validate it. With a theory worked up, he would set out, fiercely determined, to develop the new hardware it suggested. Fortunately, what his mind could imagine, his hands had the skills to make.

What Everyone Wants to Remark

There were, undeniably, those who found him acerb, stubborn, irascible. He certainly could be impatient and sharp with those he thought pretentious. He could also be jealous and secretive, as he was in the first days of his discovery of the jassid. On the other hand, I knew him to be gracious, generous, even gallant. He could pay the handsomest compliment, as he did when he told me that he often quoted an article I had written.

I think there can be little doubt that he was deeply pessimistic about things, which, I suspect, was only another way of thinking about his own life. I recall the deep melancholy of his monologue in the back of a van headed for Falling Spring Run one Sunday morning. He allowed that a trout stream had to be in the end antithetical to modern civilization. He thought our fishing would soon be done for. On the other hand, he spoke that morning with innocent pleasure at seeing a butterfly on the meadow again after DDT had effectively wiped them out. Perhaps his most powerful, much quoted public statement (it began as a paper for the Fly Fishers' Club) was on the horrendous urbanization that he saw destroying his beloved spring creeks. For a short time, in his despair, he nearly quit fishing.

On that same Sunday drive to Falling Spring, I experienced the Marinaro who has dismayed so many. I asked him about a particular interest of mine, James Leisenring, of earlier Pennsylvania fly-fishing fame. Vince was abrupt in his opinion that Leisenring was much overrated and that was that. Thrown onto the defensive, I caught myself thinking that perhaps Vince did not bear competition well. Among champs, there's never room for more than one.

He felt neglected. His important work and its culmination in the *Code* had not been fully recognized or understood. Almost as soon as the *Code* was published in 1950, I was able to buy my copy from a remainders list. Putnam had given the great book scant promotion, and Vince was disappointed. The recognition that he craved came slowly, and then, more fully, only from England. Slowly, too, the legend of the Letort, the Yellow Breeches, Big Spring, and Falling Spring spread over the angling world. By the 1970s, these streams were becoming the water one wanted to be known as having fished.

Something of Vince's difficult personality, which so many remark, may be explained by noting that while most of us buffer our expressions of opinion with hesitations, self-deprecations, even apologies, Vince's burst forth lightning fast, fully developed, like Pallas Athena from the head of Zeus. His views were instantly precise, never ambiguous, or in the least apologetic. They could almost literally take your breath away.

Many are offended or at least seriously taken aback by behavior of this sort. To face off with a Vince Marinaro was to experience a genuine and original thinker, restless and on the intellectual prowl. One had either to stand to the pressure of his personality and ideas or get out of the way. If one wanted to compete, it meant competing with the champ.

We look for soft spots, places even of weakness, in others in order to justify our affection for them. Most could find no soft spots at all in Vince Marinaro. For me, it was perhaps his capacity for an elegant and formal courtesy that I fastened on.

He tells us that he was always of a "somewhat nervous temperament." He even separated himself out from the Waltonian tradition of angling as a meditative, inner-directed activity much involved with the spirit. He spoke of his aggressive absorption in the work of angling and of angling itself as a blood sport. He thought that understanding the nature of angling as gentle and contemplative was a curious anomaly, what with the fish's very blood on our hands. He was tough-minded.

Still, my own experience was always with Marinaro the gentleman, expert in the graceful traditions of his European heritage. He was even willing to forgive my fond enthusiasm for Big Jim Leisenring.

Marinaro and the Trout Fly

It's hard to overestimate the importance of his promotion and codification of fishing with imitation ants and beetles, crickets and grasshoppers, jassids and inchworms—all the landborn insects now so common and important to international fly fishing.

Many will recall that he introduced us, in his famous *Outdoor Life* article, to the wonderful "hidden hatch" that he at first misidentified as *Caenis* but in some chagrin came correctly to know as *Tricorythodes.* The world of insect minutiae became available to us, what with Marinaro's work and the sudden availability in the 1950s of fine nylon tippets and the tiny hooks necessary for this kind of fishing.

In the *Code* he tells us how he discovered the all-important *Baetis,* that tiny mayfly that everybody had overlooked. Our fly fishing today is unthinkable without *Baetis,* our essential little Blue-Winged Olive.

He made much of witnessing the coming of an altogether new insect to American trout fishing. The Japanese beetle found its way to these shores in 1916 and steadily established itself throughout the East and Midwest. By the 1940s hoards of them were devastating crops and gardens, eating up everything in sight, and falling into trout streams. The trout, like ducks, gobbled them up. Marinaro tried a fly made by another Pennsylvanian from a coffee bean glued to a hook shank. Finding it only marginally successful, Marinaro, on the theory that the trout could not discern the thickness of the beetle's body but only an opaque outline of it, used one or two large jungle cock nails flat on a hook shank, with the added suggestion of legs, and developed a winning pattern beloved of Letort trout.

A major discovery came from his and Charlie Fox's careful, close-up examination of the Letort's surface film. They found more extremely tiny insects than they had imagined possible. Among them were the tiny jassids, leaf rollers, and their ilk. As soon as they found the jassid and saw the trout feeding heavily on them, they realized an imitation was sorely needed. The principle of the jungle-cock-nailed Japanese beetle was again the answer, though in this case requiring a much, much smaller execution.

Lightly palmering a #22 hook shank wound simply with tying silk, trimming that palmered hackle close top and bottom, then adding a small jungle cock nail flat down over the hook shank, the famous Marinaro Jassid was born. And a killer it was—if a bit too delicate structurally.

A drawback, however, to the exciting promise of terrestrials was the short fishing season back then: April 15 to July 31. Just when the insects were coming into their own in the meadow grasses, rods had to be hung up for the season or turned on the bass. Frustrated Pennsylvania anglers agitated for extended seasons and eventually got them.

I recall reading the *Code* back in its early days, when I was in Wyoming, and getting excited about these new flies. Tying up a few of those Jassids, I took them to the rough-and-ready trout in the even rougher Shoshone River, where they made fools of the trout in any little backwater where they could sit for a moment and do their stuff. The rare and beautiful jungle cock, always basic to traditional streamer and salmon flies, was now employed as other than merely handsome and decorative cheeking.

Next were the mayfly duns. Marinaro wrote that the conventional modern dry fly, suggesting a mayfly dun, developed from what he called the "wet flies" of the *Treatyse* of

1496, with later help from the flies of Charles Cotton in the seventeenth century. It was, he insisted, an illogical development—only slightly to modify a wet and call it a dry. Had the dry fly had an independent, special development all its own, which it did not, it would have looked quite different. And so, to prove his point, he invented his famous "thorax" dry-fly structure to show us how, indeed, an accurate imitation of a live, floating mayfly dun ought to look.

Through studying the trout's vision, he concluded that the dun mayfly's wing was the single most noticeable thing about the insect from the trout's point of view, and that the abdomen was of little or no importance because it did not touch the water and so could not be seen by the trout as the fly floated toward the fish's window of vision. He therefore placed large cut wings nearly halfway back on the hook shank, achieving in the process a better-balanced fly. Around the butts of the wings he wound a dubbed thorax that in a natural, he argued, would barely ride the water's surface.

Then in a masterful stroke, he wound one, sometimes two, hackles at forty-five-degree angles around that thorax and the wing butts. He wound them not around and around like a conventional stiff dry-fly collar, but in an X pattern, causing the hackle points to splay out from the hook shank fore and aft and from side to side. This fly needed fewer hackle barbules to float, and those few, he suggested, looked and behaved more like the legs of a real mayfly dun. The big, prominent wing was, in this way, made highly visible (to both fish and man). At the rear were four long, stiff, widely splayed hackle barbules raised high for outrigging tails. Up front, the dubbed thorax continued up to the eye, where everything was tied off. It's a striking fly, a fine floater, looking more like a natural, and better balanced for riding a current. But it's hard and expensive to tie. So much so that its precise form is almost never seen on the market. "Thorax-like" flies, a semblance of Marinaro's original, have found a small commercial niche.

Of all his innovative flies, Marinaro confessed that his favorite and most effective was a tiny, in-surface floating cinnamon ant with a dubbed fur dressing of his design. He suggests that it was he who discovered these myriad, almost invisible ants in the surface film of the Letort.

In 1983, Jim Bashline interviewed Marinaro.[50] It was an important audio document, in which Marinaro advanced his basic ideas with precision and charm, and in the course of the interview made the singular point that the tradition of fly fishing qua fly fishing as we have it from the British and early American traditions meant mayfly fishing, fishing to the mayfly. He noted that when a pattern bore the name of a terrestrial—and there were not many such patterns—it was unfailingly tied to look like our conventional idea of a mayfly dun. He suggested a blind spot in the theories of Halford and Marryat. One has only to think of the conventional Red Ant pattern, little different from a Royal Coachman but for its duck-quill wing of dun rather than white.

By this strategy, by defining the tradition as seriously incomplete in its theoretical base, Marinaro at a stroke opened up historical space for an alternative universe of fly fishing—to his beloved Letort terrestrials! He, in fact, opens up the necessary space within the tradition needed for his own important work. Marinaro possessed a distinctly historical consciousness, an acute, clear awareness of where he stood, or wanted to stand, in the tradition—a rare and little appreciated trait in Americans, for whom history is dull and remote. We might say that Marinaro consciously designed his role in the history of fishing the fly and wrote its self-fulfilling gospel: *A Modern Dry-fly Code.*

We have to admit that Marinaro's imaginative fly dressings are honored more in books like this than in the shops or in use on the stream. They are food for thought, if not for fish. And that may be because his flies are more prototypes in the study of tough, basic problems than the solutions themselves. They are another example of why fly fishing, at its best, is such an intensely "thinking about it" sport.

Who can doubt the importance of the grasshopper to modern fly fishing? But who today ties Marinaro's difficult butt-end-of-a-flight-quill-bodied "pontoon" hopper described in the *Code*? Who ties or fishes his thorax duns, with their big cut wings? Or who ties a mayfly spinner with a body of porcupine quill, impossible to keep from breaking off? Still, if we cannot find Marinaro's flies in the shops today and do not fish them, we nevertheless all carry flies that are what they are because of his influence and inspiration.

Marinaro, I am certain, felt a deep sense of privilege, a genuine gratitude, for his moment in the history of fly fishing. His probing mind led him to define much of that history of the fly and to play an integral role in it. He championed the literature of the fly and its tackle, insisted on its science, and developed his ideas in the field. The pity is that some of those ideas tricked him into an unfortunate dogmatism.

Coda: Marinaro resisted the use of synthetics in flies and snecked his tiny hooks.

The Fisherman

Marinaro the fisherman cannot be separated from Marinaro the rod builder. Over the course of his life he became an accomplished, self-taught worker of cane into highly unusual fly rods. They were long, stiff, and, in the estimation of some, rather awkward tools. In any case, these finely crafted rods allowed him to keep his fly out of the high grasses behind him, to reach out over the troublesome beds of elodea, and most of all to pile up big "puddle casts," giving him a good float in the tightest of spots.

This casting a puddle of loose loops of fine nylon tippet, slowly to unroll at the whim of those complex Letort currents, could not have been called, strictly speaking, a new idea. But, as with other aspects of Marinaro's achievement, he gave "a local habitation and a name," a definition and a studied technique, to what fly fishermen had been doing almost instinctively in one way or another for some time.

Although his rods were big, his reels had to be small and light for his analysis of proper casting dynamics. Interestingly enough, screwed up into the reel seat of some of his rods, after the English fashion, was a heavy turf blade—a flat spike that could be reverse-screwed back into the seat and then used to spike a rod down into the ground. So spiked, the rod stood erect, unlikely to disappear accidentally in the high grasses of meadow streams—or get stepped on.

Those who admire Marinaro's rods have wondered that they were never manufactured to the trade, his tapers revealed and made popular. I understand that there was talk of it, but that in the end, no company could or would give Marinaro the control over their production that he thought necessary if the rods were to bear his name. One suspects, also, that these rods were too specialized for beginners; and besides, there was the sudden advent of graphite as fierce competition.

With his big rods, Marinaro advocated fighting a good fish with the rod held nearly horizontal, maybe only ten degrees above. He wanted the trout to wear itself out in runs and struggles directly off the reel and from his fingertips. He argued that if the rod were held high and the line or leader departed the tip at an acute angle, the physics were against the fisherman, and tippets would snap.

He was extremely cautious in his approach to a fish. He would risk long casts over grass and water weed in order not to frighten it. Once the fish was hooked, he tried not to alarm it unduly, but rather to put it to work against the careful odds of that low rod and reel drag. Some say he played his fish longer than necessary.

Marinaro relished stalking the difficult fish, the fish rising where no one else could get at it. He relished showing bystanders how to do it. He would not infrequently offer one of these fish to a companion to try, and played the role of the bystander himself. Some say that he caught no more fish than any other competent limestone angler. That may be true, but testimony holds that he caught more of those "impossible" fish than anyone else. Those were the fish he wanted, the ones that interested him.

The last time I saw Vince was on the lower Letort, newly restored to ecological health, below Carlisle. A half dozen of us, including my wife, to whom he was nicely solicitous, were visiting lazily on the bridge when someone noticed a good fish rising a couple hundred feet downstream. We all agreed that Vince should go after it and show us how it's done. Vince accepted the invitation and took off. Into his seventies by then and braced on his ugly broom-handle-and-wire-loop combination landing net and wading staff, he ever so slowly worked his way into position for that trout. I thought he would never get there and nearly lost interest. Once in place, though, he began effortlessly to unwind one of his great long casts, putting a little Olive over the fish, and had him. A lovely fifteen-inch brown—a memorable performance.

Marinaro practiced catch-and-release, knowing well that our fishing depended on it, but he loved to eat fish, too. So, no trout was automatically safe in his hands, although the odds were highly in its favor.

Building on the work of G.E.M. Skues, Marinaro came to know fully the ways in which trout rise to a fly. Over several years he painstakingly studied and photographed every variety of rise form. His 1976 *In the Ring of the Rise*,[51] with its careful analysis and astonishing photographs of every detail of the rising event, is Vincent Marinaro's other invaluable literary and technical contribution to the sport, a beautiful and important book.

Compensations

If Vincent Marinaro never felt adequately recognized for his great contribution to fly fishing, he surely had the grand experience of it. There was the long association with Charlie Fox, who had early purchased land in Carlisle along the Letort and lived there. Only later did Marinaro buy land, to be known as "Vince's Meadow," close upstream from Fox. Both were accomplished anglers, writers, and innovators, sharing a deep scientific dedication, yet they were quite different from each other. Fox was deeply interested in his work as an editor and in casting hand-carved cedar plugs off tournament reels from long, custom bait-casting rods to smallmouths in the nearby Susquehanna. He may have been as interested in flies for his beloved bass as for the trout down in his backyard. At least, Marinaro fretted that he was.

There is some indication that late in their careers they drew apart for awhile. Marinaro may have felt at a loss in the face of his old friend's bassing. Fox knew well enough about the ups and downs of this "stubborn Italian" friend of his with whom, lying prone in the grasses of their meadows and watching their feeding trout, they developed Vince's revolutionary flies and new techniques. They made bold efforts together in fish culture—working, for instance, to transplant (unsuccessfully in the long run) the green drake *Ephemera guttalata* into the Letort. Together they fashioned spawning redds of imported gravel in the Letort silts. They applied all the science they could to their sport. Up to a point.

The late Don Ebright, then a lad whom Marinaro sometimes took fishing, recalls how he was enjoined by the old master never "to try to overwhelm the fish with technology." Though Vince may never have fished a graphite rod, he had as little good to say for them as he did about plastics in flies. The science of fishing is rich, but the mysteries of it abide our question.

In 1980, President Jimmy Carter, a passionate convert to fly fishing, convened a weekend-long meeting of fly-fishing luminaries at Camp David. Marinaro accepted the president's invitation with real satisfaction and became a close fishing friend of Carter's, meeting with him on several occasions. The Marinaro Collection contains a wonderful photograph of Vince with his pointed finger in President Carter's face.[52] Risky business surely with a president.

Marinaro mused that he had had to wait twenty-five years for the *Code* to receive the distinction it deserved in a new edition.[53] For it, in 1970, he contributed "A Backward Look," a new introduction. This essay seems to me the finest thing to come from his pen. It has none of the tensions, none of the insistence or edginess, of his earlier work. It is an old man looking back on his life in some serenity and throwing yet more light on it.

He had doted on his fame and felt he had much to prove—as much to himself as to others. Perhaps he had the most to prove to those immigrant parents and the great expectations they must have had for their small son, who must have felt that he had to grow big indeed if he was to be grown up at all.

The Letort Regulars, that gang of talented local anglers who regularly plied the stream and were buddies of Vince and Charlie, tell a wonderful story: Vince and Bill Fritz were in Michigan to fish the Au Sable, a river that Vince had declared the ideal trout stream. They were resting of an afternoon on the river's edge when Vince picked a rather nondescript rock from the water and began a grand apostrophe, a paean, in its praise—how this extraordinary object had come into being, all that it had witnessed over the ages, etc. Fritz felt a bit embarrassed, not knowing how to respond. To make matters worse, Vince insisted on presenting the "noble stone" to Fritz, who hadn't the faintest notion what to do with it and so thrust it into his waders and hauled it ignobly home.

Once home, and the story bruited about, Fritz knew that something had to be done with this rock, and the idea occurred to him to present it right back to Vince with all the ceremony he could muster at a Trout Unlimited banquet in Vince's honor. Everybody there enjoyed yet another laugh over another of their many shared "gotcha" jokes. Not to be outdone, Marinaro soon found occasion to present it back to Fritz, to everyone's increasing glee. And so it went back and forth between them, this ordinary chunk of rock in which so much significance had been vested.

And here the story rests while Vincent C. Marinaro, in his seventy-fifth year, on March 2, 1986, dies a hard death of leukemia in Newville, Pennsylvania. His secular funeral was held in New Cumberland, Pennsylvania.

This, however, was not the end. In the old days before the fishing season was extended past July 31, it was the custom of the Letort Regulars to meet on the stream that last evening of the season for a ceremony they called "the Last Supper."

In March 1986, the Regulars held a special Last Supper in the great man's honor right there in his own meadow. From the railroad trestle, Vince's ashes were dropped into the stream that he had made legend.

This rite was soon followed by a third ceremony: the tossing of the Fritz-Marinaro Noble Stone into the Letort Spring Run.

Beyond the fun of Marinaro's noble stone, there lies a hint of the potential for nobility in all things, of how an ordinary stone from deep in our particular waters can, in fact, be a touchstone making the nobility of things manifest. Like Vincent Marinaro, we have only to find it, take it up, and loose its transforming virtues.[54]

Big Jim Leisenring, the Grand Old Man

The flies I tied while waiting to be old enough for World War II were thick, overdressed, and opaque. The only theory behind them, if you could call it that, was to imitate the commercial wet flies I saw in the stores—and to tie them with small, neat heads.

Then James E. Leisenring entered my life, and my flies were never the same. My late, lamented friend Alan Olson, later an archaeologist at the University of Denver, was fortunate enough back then to have an Uncle Everett in New York City who did petit-point and sent his nephew bits of fishing stuff to feed his growing love of fly fishing. One Christmas before we went away to war, there came a small, thin book called *The Art of Tying the Wet Fly* by that splendid old Pennsylvanian James Leisenring, at that time altogether unknown to us kids. But we were a reformation ready to happen, and not without a certain youthful snobbish interest in things eastern.

And so Leisenring's book became our instruction and inspiration. Our flies became smaller, sparse, translucent, more delicate. They began to exhibit that classic profile, with wings of starling-quill slips sweeping low over the backs of precisely shaded bodies dubbed on Persall's Finest Gossamer silk. In the water these flies would move somewhat in the way of real insects. We discovered a whole new world of fly-tying material and acquired a cultural hero in the process.

Big Jim, as he was known to his friends, was an authentic Pennsylvania Dutchman, native-born in Seidersville, Pennsylvania, near Allentown, on November 27, 1878. He stood well over six feet, had a commanding presence, and never married, living instead, most of the time, with his mother and sister. His life centered closely around the Delaware Valley, though he traveled extensively all over the continent in his pursuit of trout. Traveled rather more, in fact, than we might expect of a toolmaker for Bethlehem Steel, more than we might expect of a man who in many ways suggests the rugged, blue-collar worker who, faithful to work and family, keeps to his home.

Yes, if Vincent Marinaro suggests the intellectual, and if there is something of the aesthete in Theodore Gordon, smack in the middle of this triumvirate of great Pennsylvanians is the working-class Leisenring. Modest, self-effacing Leisenring, who refused to promote himself as a celebrity of the fly. How profoundly different he appears from the aggressive angling expert/celebrity of today.

With little formal education, he taught himself what he needed to know and grew highly sophisticated in a down-to-earth way. He became the center of an important group of angler-admirers and followers who dubbed themselves Leisenring's "Twelve Disciples"—their dozen names reading like a who's who of the eastern fly-fishing establishment. Their headquarters was on Big Jim's beloved Broadheads Creek, at the famed Rapids Hotel in Analomink in the Poconos. There they constituted themselves the Broadheads Forest and Stream Fishing Club, James E. Leisenring, founder and past master.

He was highly regarded in the United States and perhaps even more so in England, where the famous founder of the nymph G.E.M. Skues touted Jim's achievements and his flies at the legendary Fly Fishers' Club of London. He and Skues had a considerable correspondence, each winning the other's admiration and approbation. They were on highly similar historical wavelengths, with their advocacy of sunken flies—the

James Leisenring.

wet, the nymph—and how to tie and fish them. Interesting that both of these important figures came upon the scene just when the currents ran so squarely against them, for this was the time of the ascendancy of the dry fly. Skues was, in fact, driven off his own dearly loved water on the Itchen, where it was decided that his nymphs, his sunken flies, were too uncouth, if not unethical, to be tolerated any longer.

Fellow Pennsylvanian and angler Vernon S. Hidy began to pester Leisenring to write a book about his flies and how to tie them, to set it all down for posterity. Leisenring resisted until Hidy agreed to help write the book from Jim's dictation and notes. And so, in 1941, Dodd, Mead & Co. published *The Art of Tying the Wet Fly,* that wonderful little book that came to mean so much to Alan Olson and me. The book was well received, but did not sweep the field of angling publications, precisely because the drift of things at that time so favored the dry fly. This smacked somewhat of class warfare, the dry fly being hailed as more elegant, sporting, and interestingly difficult, and, therefore, clearly superior.

Slowly, however, over the years, those of us lucky enough to have a copy of the book and to have been improved by it thought of ourselves as extending the Discipleship where and when we could. We bided our time, with our Leisenring wets in our boxes or our books.

Then, in 1960, the March and April *Sports Illustrated* featured Leisenring, his flies, and his methods in a big four-part weekly series, disappointing only because it was too much directed at the neophyte. But again it was Vernon Hidy's enterprise in these articles that rescued Big Jim's reputation as an American master. Change was in the air, and that change read "soft-hackle flies."

But not in time to do this great classic fisher of the wet fly any good. He died penniless on September 30, 1951, at seventy-two in an Allentown hospital—so broke that a brother was forced to sell Jim's fly books to help pay for his funeral.

It has been my good fortune to see two of those fly books and hold them in my hands. They are rather small, old-fashioned, simple folds of snap-closing leather and parchment, with inner leaves of felt holding his little flies in neat rows. Leisenring's name is carefully inked inside.

Having always believed that fly books and boxes are deeply personal containers of intimate psychological stuff, I ventured to pry into the dead man's secrets, to read the notes that these old fly books contained in their recesses. I tried to feel their talismanic quality. I suppose this essay is a report on what I experienced.

There's surely something melancholy about it all, a melancholy I don't feel about either Gordon or Marinaro. It's painful to me that Marinaro was so quick to dismiss Big Jim, who had meant so much to me and to Alan. It was disappointing that he could not have died more widely known and generally esteemed, instead of running down into obscurity. Not until 1993 was a local memorial ceremony held in his honor on the Little Lehigh Creek at Allentown. A plaque was placed on a large rock at the river's edge, and Ernest Schwiebert delivered the oration on Big Jim to those, like me, who think of themselves as Leisenring's latter-day disciples.

Happily, Leisenring is being heard from again. His name now dots current angling literature. We hear of him as the originator of the now popular soft-hackle flies. We read, here and there, of the "Leisenring lift," with which he teased a fish to strike. Yet this is but a pale reflection of his fuller contribution. Leisenring taught us how to think anew about fly-tying materials, about hackle, not just from barnyard fowl, but from all manner of birds providing all manner of texture, color, tint, and sizes for reimagining the wet fly. After hackles, he emphasized carefully mixed dubbings of exact shade and translucency. In fact, that word *translucency* might well be his watchword.

How the fly looked when wet was all-important. When dry, it could give no reliable indication of what a wetting in the stream would do to it to make a trout love it. The famous Tups Nymph, for instance, in his estimation the best of all nymphs, is a beautiful thing, with its primrose yellow silk abdomen and pretty pinkish tups wool thorax. But what is it like when wet? That's another thing entirely. Those appealing and delicate shades blend into what he felt was a nearly universal nymphal look—at least to the fish. In the case of the Tups, he taught us how *not* to wrap the body of primrose silk buttonhole twist over waxed tying thread lest in the water that opaque thread kill the desired translucency. Dub that body over bare steel! He was one of the first in my experience to insist that the color of tying silk on which a fur body is dubbed is as important as the dubbing color itself. The silk color must show through and contribute to the overall effect of the body. Sometimes I think that primrose yellow must have been his favorite color.

Leisenring taught us to collect plumages everywhere and all the time. And when we have a material that we know to be exactly right in a dressing, we are to insist on it, demand it of ourselves, as he so rigorously did. After Leisenring we can never look at peacock herl in the same way again. We are forever scouting out that scarce bronze cast of herl that he insisted was so superior to the ordinary greenish stuff.

For what may well be Leisenring's signature fly, the Brown (or Red) Hackle, the bronze herl is essential. He calls for his dressing to be tied with claret tying silk, no tail, a bronze peacock herl body ribbed with narrow gold tinsel, and a hackle of furnace. The claret silk will provide a nice red head. Almost from the inception of fly fishing, the red or brown hackle has been most basic. And who today would argue with the proposition that, in combination with peacock herl, a good brown or, still better, a furnace hackle is the most productive of all?

Leisenring wanted a fly to move in the water in a lifelike way. Proper action was paramount. The hackles had to breathe, the dubbing glisten like a nymph's pumping gills. And, of course, his flies were two or three sizes smaller than the flies that tradition had handed him. I think that only the aristocratic George La Branche was at that time insisting on a fly's action as the measure of all things as insistently as Leisenring.

I also believe that Leisenring was the first in print with the dubbing loop, the capture of fur between two strands of silk that are then twisted together into what is tantamount to a yarn. For Alan Olson and me, what with Leisenring's championing Persalls' Finest Gossamer tying silk, the dubbing loop was a major discovery.

The trick of his wet-fly tying method lies in tying in the hackle first, pointing it away to the right from the hook's eye while the tail and body parts are completed. With the tying thread hanging away to the left, the hackle is then wound, maybe only two turns, back to that point where body and tying silk are met. The silk is then wound forward through the hackle, where a perfectly clean, level base awaits on which to tie the wing. Somehow, it works wonderfully, producing that classic profile that we all admire and strive for—especially on sproat-bend hooks. As far as I know, only Leisenring and Skues advocated this method.

He was known to tie flies on the stream as needed, being as he was a careful student of stream life and ready for anything new. His fishing vest was remodeled out of an old hunting coat and augmented with a very large wicker creel for manly trout. Out of that vest he could produce a variety of tying materials and without a vice tie most anything on the spot. Once, in 1932, when visiting Colorado's South Platte with two old friends and a boy, paying for their keep at the hotel in South Platte by providing the hotel with trout, Big Jim sat beside the stream, tying flies in his big fingers to the amazement of fourteen-year-old David Miller of Denver. Jim observed to the starstruck boy that he should "always wade softly and carry a big stick."

Dave Miller to this day still fishes the South Platte every Tuesday and Thursday and remembers that the big Pennsylvania master would willingly go dry when fish were taking on the surface, but let them slow down a bit and he was back underneath with his wet or nymph—"a sweet and pleasant man," as Dave remembers him.

We can imagine him now, alongside a run in the Broadheads or the Platte, casting his wets upstream, urging them to sink to just the right depth as they come past him, then, by lifting his rod, initiating the famous Leisenring Lift, bringing the fly toward the surface just as a nymph rises from the bottom to drive trout crazy.

The Last of It

Ghost Lake

If a lake should disappear, where might it go?

Just north of town, atop a mesa fingering down from the foothills of the Rockies, is a small reservoir where I caught my very first fish sixty years ago. The map shows it in a light blue tint as Mesa Reservoir, but we knew it back then as Deggues Lake. For a long time I'd wanted to see this lake again, maybe even fish it, this special water where all this "fishing business" began so long ago.

The lake, surrounded now by county open space, is no longer accessible by car. And so my wife and I, one fine winter's day, took our lunch and walked the mile of old road to reach it. It was a grand walk on a grand day to find once again that special lake—or rather, where the lake ought to have been.

Because there was no lake. There was its dried-up basin, its shoreline denoted by scrub willow and ancient, massive dead cottonwoods on the east dike. But the lake, the reservoir, had disappeared completely. And Farmer's Ditch, which had brought water from the mountains for storage here against the farming needs of summer, had obviously long been dry.

The old warm-water lake had held bluegill, crappie, and bass in abundance; now there were only native prairie grasses, gone to winter gold, with scrub junipers here and there. Dismayed and at a loss, I hardly knew what to think or do next.

So, Betty and I walked the perimeter of the missing lake to the rocky dike at the east end, clambering over the silvered trunks and limbs of fallen cottonwoods, gaunt, skeletal remains of their former majesty. Among them was a comfortable place to eat lunch where we could look out to the west, across the dry lake to the mountains in the near distance. It was a quiet, sun-drenched Colorado winter midday to be remembered.

I could see just where on the northwest shore the Schons family had brought me on my first fishing trip so very long ago. The three kids and their dad had more-or-less-proper tackle, but I had only a brand-new hand line, got at Woolworth's for five cents, and a can of worms. In memory, I easily recovered the excitement of it all, along with the frustration of my inability to hurl the line, bobber, sinker, and big Cincinnati-Bass hook with worm more than a dozen feet or so out into the lake. Still, the worm, when it hit the water, drew lots of those half-dollar-sized sunnies. It was nibble, nibble, run away and back again, and nibble some more. I caught a few, but with that hand line they were extremely difficult to hook.

Hand line on frame

The usefulness of a rod became immediately apparent, and I resolved to have one. Rod or no rod, though, the day was a revelation that would determine much of what my life would become. It changed everything and utterly.

I wondered about all these things as Betty and I talked of our lives together and ate our lunch. But most of all, I wondered about those sunfish that had to have perished with the lake. How did they die—in some sort of holocaust of accelerating suffocation? And did they just lie there then, those desiccated corpses of sunfish and bass, bronzed in the baking sun, their eyeballs a feast for soaring hawks? I could envision them lying there rotting, all over the basin of the lake.

But I could see beyond that. I could see the air full of the radiant, jeweled bodies of all those little fish, rising into the sky from all over the wasted lake like myriad gilded butterflies, caught up in the sun and disappearing off into the western empyrean.

Might it not have been that way? Must they, rather, have merely lain there, carrion and rotting flesh? I choose to think that those fish I knew back then as a twelve-year-old boy were taken up into the skies in a marvelous transformation, like ghosts, to live again in a ghost lake of my heart. I choose to believe that, for better or for worse, nothing is ever really lost in this world, and that we can and must choose between the forces of corruption and decay and the potential of all created things for "a sea change into something rich and strange."

The Fisherman

Hurrying down Boulder Canyon early one sullen spring morning and just rounding a bend, I saw him, down in the creek, a fisherman working his flies in silhouette over the rough water. I saw him only for an instant. A spectral image in black cut into the silvered water beyond him. He seemed

from another time and place, but I knew him at once, re-membered him.

I wanted to give him an old Boulder name, that of some onetime habitué of Boulder Creek. He might have been E. B. Edwards, Charlie Sundquist, or Nick Schons. Maybe he was "One-Armed" Billie Marquette, Bill Smith, Al Olson, or Lasses Ralston. Perhaps he was my Uncle Art. In any case, this was the original, the model, the archetype that flashes into consciousness and reminds us of sources, beginnings, and raises floods of sensation and memory.

By naming him, I thought I might perhaps anchor myself more securely into the legend of this landscape, my native watershed. Forms and images like this, I know, are as old as time and have this powerful way of taking on a local habita-tion and a name. But, in this instant, no single name seemed right. The image remained simply, the Fisherman.

That vision of the Fisherman on the creek—a mere in-stant—sent shivers through me that were slow to subside. See-ing a ghost, I thought, must be like this.

The Irish poet William Butler Yeats saw the Fisherman, too, in the mountains of Connemara. This archetype invaded Yeats's imagination and poems and became a dominant symbol of rigor, integrity, controlled passion, manhood. A symbol of what might be, amid all the spiritual squalor, intellectual sloth, hatred, and ugliness that the poet found in the Irish life of his time. The solitary angler became the symbol of what was, perhaps, Yeats's only hope for his native land.

In 1919, this spectral angler appeared in the poem "The Fisherman."

> I can see him still,
> The freckled man who goes
> To a grey place on a hill
> In grey Connemara clothes
> At dawn to cast his flies,
>
> . . .
>
> This wise and simple man.

The poem proceeds to catalog the Irishmen of Yeats's despair: cravens, drunks, and fools, who spoil all they touch. Then the poem returns for solace to the Fisherman:

> Imagining a man,
> And his sun-freckled face,
> And grey Connemara cloth,
> Climbing up to a place
> Where stone is dark under froth,
> And the down-turn of his wrist
> When the flies drop in the stream;
> A man who does not exist,
> A man who is but a dream;
> And cried, "Before I am old
> I shall have written him one
> Poem maybe as cold
> And passionate as the dawn.

In the poem "The Tower," he writes of this fisherman again. But this time we encounter him among younger fishermen, in whom the poet invests whatever hope he has, fishermen

That climb the streams until
The fountains leap, and at dawn
Drop their cast at the side
of dripping stone;

. . .

I leave both faith and pride
To young upstanding men
Climbing the mountain side,
That under bursting dawn
They may drop a fly.

The transformation is wonderful. The old Fisherman, a dark and melancholy silhouette, whether on a Connemara mountainside or in Boulder Canyon, is now in a company of young men, bursting into life like the dawn.

The great thing is that what is old and exhausted can be transformed into what is young and new and full of hope—that the entire phenomenon can be memorialized and kept alive in a poem "as cold and passionate as the dawn."

As I write these words, the very wonder of words themselves, of language, of the propensity and need for words to make the poem quite overwhelms me. And I'm suddenly struck by what now seems so obvious: that fishing and language are somehow inextricably bonded, that the act of fishing is fulfilled, perhaps begun, in the act of language. Yes, that's it! The Essential Fish, the Fish that every fish expresses, is drawn up only in a net of words, into the Poem.

Regardless of how frustrating and unsatisfactory the confused events of our lives become, whether in Connemara or Colorado, there's promise of another way: that ancient, youthful angler stands there still in the cold grey dawn, casting his flies from the past into the future to a prey that is not prey at all, but the end of a quest for renewed life of the spirit.

I leave off these essays now, leave them to the young and full of hope, to those grandchildren to make of them what they will. But I leave them, too, for that completed Fisherman whom I saw in that instant of vision on Boulder Creek. I dare to imagine that in some peculiar way, in these pages, he may continue to wade and cast his flies into an ever new dawn.

Acknowledgments

I am indebted to that master haberdasher Court Dixon and to entrepreneurial attorney Chris Sullivan, both past presidents of the Boulder Flycasters, a chapter of Trout Unlimited, who gave me the opportunity to begin writing regularly about fishing early in my retirement. In so many ways of the spirit, I'm indebted to Lou Feierabend, who invented the SuperZ ferrule, built my five-strip rods so long ago, and demonstrated the kind of life we ought all try to live. And to Karl Harper of Laramie, who read and marked my pages so well and got me up and running. My neighbor and accomplished graphic artist Michael Signorella has been of great help. The noted John Betts of Denver has been the sort of inspiration I most needed and treasure. I've been elegantly supported by fine editors: Art Scheck at *Fly Tyer;* Dave Foster and Jim Babb at *Gray's Sporting Journal;* Margot Page, who let me into the pages of *The American Fly Fisher;* and to her successor as editor of *TAFF* Kathleen Achor, wonderful and indispensable. And new friend and fellow angler Luther Wilson, formerly of the University Press of Colorado, who agreed to publish this book. Thanks also to copy editor Debbie Korte. Finally, I should be nowhere without the unerring eye and intelligence brought to bear first on my work in the theatre and now on these essays by my wife Betty Wickstrom. She brings her own fifty-plus years of fishing the fly to the formation of this book.

Notes

1. My edition of Bergman was published by Knopf (New York: 1952), my edition of Marbury by Wellfleet Press (Edison, NJ: 1988).

2. The Major Pitcher is listed but not illustrated in the 1936 catalog for the Weber Life-like Fly Co. of Stevens Point, Wisconsin. J. Edson Leonard gives the dressing, complete with silk body, in his *Flies* (New York: Barnes, 1950). When and how it became the "Major" Pitcher is not known.

3. Ray Bergman, *Trout* (New York: Knopf, 1952), and Paul Schmookler and Ingrid Sils, *Forgotten Flies* (Millis, MA: The Complete Sportsman, 1999).

4. The best source of the finest lamb's wool, from which the lanolin has been removed, readying it to be dyed any color, is the special batting used by ballet dancers, who place it between their toes to lessen the terrible pain of dancing. Any dance/performance supply shop will provide it.

5. The Skues Formula: wool "from the indispensable part of a tup," the fine pinkish fur from the poll of a hare's ear, cream-colored seal, the lemon yellow combings from a spaniel, and a bit of red mohair or seal.

6. Revised from the original, "That First Time," as it appeared in *Gray's Sporting Journal* (February 1993): 120.

7. L. B. France, *With Rod and Line in Colorado Waters,* first published under the pen name "Bourgeois" (1884; reprint, Boulder, CO: Pruett, 1996).

8. "Eros" here refers to the Freudian concept, not the character in Greek mythology.

9. Colorado's fourth cutthroat, the yellowfin *Oncorhynchus clarki macdonaldi* (the other three are the Colorado River, the Rio Grande, and the greenback) is held to be extinct, wiped out by rainbow hybridization.

It was indigenous to the small area of Twin Lakes near Leadville, Colorado, and lived happily there side by side with the greenback without hybridization—until the advent of the rainbow. The yellowfin kept to the depths and grew to eight or nine pounds, whereas the greenback preferred shallow waters and streams and stayed small. Curiously, yellowfin were sent to France and from there to Germany and not heard of thereafter. Professor Behnke has wondered if a yellowfin may not have survived in some remote water, just waiting to be found.

10. Dr. William Howard Rickard, Jr., is retired from the Pacific Northwest National Laboratories in Richland, Washington. He now fishes the westslope cutthroat and steelhead, continues his research, and develops special teaching projects for the National Laboratories and the Richland public school system.

11. See the bastard Falconbridge's searing indictment of "commodity" in Shakespeare's *King John,* Act II, sc. i.

12. Jose Ortega y Gasset, *Meditations on Hunting* (New York: Charles Scribner & Sons, 1972), 32–33.

13. Ibid., 31.

14. Ibid.

15. Ernest Hemingway, *The Old Man and the Sea* (New York: Charles Scribner & Sons, 1972), 54.

16. Harry Middleton, *Rivers of Memory* (Boulder, CO: Pruett, 1993), 31.

17. Emile Mâle, *The Gothic Image: Religious Art in France in the Thirteenth Century* (New York: Harpers, 1958), 380.

18. It was McDonald's pivotal research and writing that in the 1940s restored Theodore Gordon to our historical memory and honor. Unfortunately, Gordon had neglected to put his ideas and experience into book form, leaving it all to the vagaries of magazine articles and letters here and there that were easily lost and forgotten.

19. John McDonald, *Quill Gordon* (New York: Knopf, 1972).

20. Act IV, Sc. iv, 70–110.

21. McDonald, 6.

22. Mark Browning, *Haunted by Waters* (Athens, OH: Ohio University Press, 1998), 27.

23. For many years, the opening day of Colorado's fishing season was May 25.

24. The Irish fly fisherman "puts up" a fly when he chooses a pattern and attaches it to his cast (leader).

25. Nymph, dun, and spinner (larva, sub-imago, and imago) are the three developmental stages of a mayfly's life. The Irish angler says that the hatch of flies is "coming down" when they appear.

26. Irish anglers often prefer wind and rain for the best fishing and have a saying that they want only enough blue in the sky to make themselves a shirt.

27. Dectine (Dek-tin-a) was Cuchulain's (Cu-hoo-lin) mother. In one stage of the hero's conception, she is said to have swallowed a Mayfly. Mayfly is a generic term in America but indicates exclusively *Ephemera danica* in Ireland.

28. When 150 envious queens mutilated the wife of Lugaidh Redstripe, Cuchulain killed them all at the Ford of the Woman Slaughter. Lugaidh's queen Derbforgaill had a stronger stream of urine than the other women and was therefore more desirable to men than they.

29. A student once wrote in an essay for me, "Cuchulain's life is woman's work." He was uncertain what he meant.

30. Lugh, the God of the Sun, and chief in the Irish pantheon, was Cuchulain's divine father.

31. On his way to his last battle, Cuchulain was waylaid by the witch daughters of Calatin, who offered him a feast of dog flesh. Cuchulain was under *Geasa*, or taboo, not to eat the flesh of dogs, nor to refuse any feast. As a result of eating this feast, he was so fatally compromised that his enemies had an easier time against him when he defended Ulster, the North, singlehanded.

32. Mortally wounded, Cuchulain, with his enemies still at bay, walked to a lake nearby with his bowels in his hands to drink and wash himself. He then tied himself upright to a pillar-stone to die. Only when a raven came to perch on his shoulder did his enemies know that he was dead and dare to approach and dismember him.

33. Ferdia was Cuchulain's best friend and brother-in-arms. In the great Tain, "The Cattle Raid of Cooney," he was on the side of Ireland and fought against Cuchulain and Ulster. They fought for many days, comforting and caring for each other's wounds by night. In the end, Cuchulain killed Ferdia with the *Gae Bolga,* the ultimate weapon that Cuchulain alone possessed and used to such tragic ends. He was never justified in using it. It was a kind of spear that when thrust broke out into terrible darts.

34. When Conla, Cuchulain's son by Aoife, arrived in Ireland from Scotland, Cuchulain killed him with the *Gae Bolga* without knowing

until too late who the younger hero really was.

35. Emer was Cuchulain's wife, an ideal wife and woman who had to bear Cuchulain's constant infidelity and neglect.

36. Ned is my friend Colonel Edward Cusack, then chief of Irish Army Intelligence, now retired, who took me fishing on the Kells Blackwater that day in May.

37. The Shannon is an imperfect watershed, some of its water at its sources flowing north.

38. The great epic *Tain Bo Cuailgne* recounts the effort of Queen Maeve of Connacht to rustle the great Brown Bull of Ulster in order to match the White-horned Bull owned by her husband Ailill, who taunted his wife with his grand possession. At the end of the *Tain,* after days of struggle, the Ulster Bull killed the Connacht (Irish) Bull, leaving parts of him all over the hills of Ireland, before dying in turn.

39. The Wharfe is a principal river in the dales of Yorkshire. My host was Leslie Warnett of the Red Lion in the village of Burnsall, which lies on that river.

40. Ernest Schwiebert, "Legend and Letort," in *The Complete Schwiebert: A Treasury of Trout Fishing From Around the World* (New York: Truman Talley Books/Dutton, 1990), 63–64. For many years, Pennsylvania's trout season was from April 15 to July 31.

41. *The Complete Fly-Fisherman: The Notes and Letters of Theodore Gordon,* ed. John McDonald (New York: Charles Scribner's Sons, 1947), 466.

42. Ibid., 509.

43. Ibid., 33.

44. Ibid., 154.

45. More than fifty years have passed since John McDonald and New York's Theodore Gordon Flyfishers Club set out to recover the neglected Gordon. The first edition of *The Complete Fly-Fisherman: The Notes and Letters of Theodore Gordon,* collected and edited by McDonald, appeared in 1947.

46. Vincent Marinaro, *A Modern Dry-fly Code* (New York: G. P. Putnam & Sons, 1950).

47. Joe Brooks, "Jassids—New Approach to Fly Fishing," *Outdoor Life* (March 1958): 52–80.

48. Vincent C. Marinaro, "The Hidden Hatch," *Outdoor Life* (July 1969): 48–82.

49. *Limestone Legends: The Papers and Recollections of the Fly Fishers' Club of Harrisburg, 1947–1997,* eds. Norm Shires and Jim Gilford (Mechanicsburg, PA: Stackpole Books, 1997), passim.

50. "60 Minutes Fly Fishing with Vince Marinaro," audiotape interview with Marinaro conducted by Jim Bashline, Program One, KAP Studios, Inc., Philadelphia, PA., 1983.

51. Vincent C. Marinaro, *In the Ring of the Rise* (New York: Crown, 1976).

52. The Marinaro Collection of tackle and materials was entrusted to Marinaro's son Sebastian. Prior to Sebastian's death at forty-eight of a melanoma in 1997, he had sought the aid of Don Ebright in managing the collection. Ebright then continued to aid Sebastian's wife, Margaret, with the collection. It has been acquired by the Pennsylvania Fly Fishing Center and Museum at Allenberry, Pennsylvania, Tom Wittle, president.

53. Vincent Marinaro, *A Modern Dry-fly Code* (New York: Crown, 1970).

54. I am indebted to Richard L. Henry of Lebanon, Pennsylvania. Without him this essay would have been impossible. At first, because Henry had long known and fished with Marinaro and is a writer himself, I urged that he write the essay or that we write it together. But he preferred to help me. Also, the cooperation of the late Don Ebright of Camp Hill, Pennsylvania, from his boyhood a fishing companion of Marinaro's, was invaluable. Marinaro's eldest child, Vincentia Czotter of Middletown, Pennsylvania, has been of great help, as has her cousin and Marinaro's nephew, Julius Marinaro of Bennett, Colorado.

My association with Marinaro was limited to a time when I was on faculty at Franklin and Marshall College in Lancaster, Pennsylvania.

Author and Composer

Gordon Wickstrom is a native of Boulder, Colorado, a WWII navy veteran, and a graduate of the University of Colorado. He began his career in Wyoming—teaching, making theatre, and fishing. Holding a Ph.D. from Stanford University, he was a professor of drama and department head at Franklin and Marshall College in Pennsylvania and an occassional director and actor with The Colorado Shakespeare Festival. He retired back to Boulder in 1991.

A sometime critic of dramatic art and literature, he now thinks and writes like a critic of fishing—as well as acts, directs, and produces theatre. He has written about fishing for *Gray's Journal, Fly Tyer,* and *Angler's Journal* and is a regular contributor to *The American Fly Fisher.* He has published a linear display of the chronology of fly fishing, now in a second edition, and writes and circulates quarterly *The Bouldercreek Angler,* a gazette for those who fish, and *The Bouldercreek Actor,* a gazette for those who make theatre.

John Patrick Thomas is a native of Denver, Colorado. For five summers he studied composition with Darius Milhaud and Charles Jones at the Aspen Music School. Thomas holds two degrees from the University of California at Berkeley. Since 1971, he has pursued a singing career in Europe as a countertenor with a special interst in new and early music. Currently living in Hamburg, Germany, he divides his time between teaching singing and composing. His setting of "The Letort Spring Run" is not his first collaboration with Gordon Wickstrom. As a high school student in Powell, Wyoming, Thomas studied English literature and drama with Wickstrom, who also directed Thomas's first opera in 1961.